Before The Application

Before The Application
How to Become the Ideal College Candidate
A Step-by-Step Guide to Making Each Year of High School Count

GEARY WOOLFOLK
with Dedra R. Woolfolk, PhD

Before The Application
Copyright © 2020 Geary Woolfolk

ISBN: 978-1-7361255-0-2 (paperback)
ISBN: 978-1-7361255-1-9 (ebook)

All rights reserved. No part of this book may be reproduced, stored, or transmitted by any means—whether auditory, graphic, mechanical, or electronic—without written permission of both publisher and author, except in the case of brief excerpts used in critical articles and reviews. Unauthorized reproduction of any part of this work is illegal and is punishable by law.

Because of the dynamic nature of the Internet, any web addresses or links contained in this book may have changed since publication and may no longer be valid. The views expressed in this work are solely those of the author and do not necessarily reflect the views of the publisher, and the publisher hereby disclaims any responsibility for them.

To Barbara J Woolfolk,
the greatest mother in the world, for always
believing in me and consistently supporting me!

Contents

Acknowledgements ix
Foreword xi

Before We Get Started. 1

Planning for Success 9
    The Guide. 9
    The Wheels. 12
    The Plan. 14
    The Execution (Keys to Success) 19

Ninth Grade—Buying In 23
    The Fundamentals—Laying the Groundwork. 26
    Freshman Essentials—Taking Flight. 32
    Freshman Timeline—Starting with Purpose. 49

Tenth Grade—Planning for the "Next". 77
    The Fundamentals—Building on the Foundation. .. 81
    Sophomore Essentials—Taking Control 86
    College Prep Courses—Choosing Wisely 91
    Sophomore Timeline—Generating Momentum 102

Eleventh Grade—Putting a Stamp on Your Brand 125
    The Fundamentals—Solidifying the Core. 127
    Junior Essentials—Taking Responsibility 133
    Junior Timeline—Remain Steadfast 142

The College Application 155
Twelfth Grade—Finishing Strong. 181
    The Fundamentals—Final Touches. 184
    Senior Essentials—Taking Care. 185
    Senior Timeline—Focus on the Details. 187
Post-Graduation—Starting College Strong 211
    Post-Graduation Essentials—Taking it Forward 214
    Post-Graduation Timeline—Next Level Planning. 217
My Farewell. 225
Notes 227
Index 231

Acknowledgements

I had no idea what I was getting myself into when I started writing this book. There is no way that I could have made it without significant assistance from several important people. More than anything, I thank God for the opportunity to be in a position to share this book with you!

My children are the basis for this book, and I thank them for allowing me to share so much of their story. Their commitment to the plan for their educational pursuits made the job of preparing them for college so much easier for their mother and me. I do have to give special acknowledgement to Brian for the considerable amount of time he spent poring over every word with me to ensure my message was understood.

This book would not have been possible without the countless hours of support from Gramisha Hernandez. I cannot say thank you enough for leading this blind man to water. I did not know how to get to my destination, and I am in your debt for guiding me all the way through to the end.

Thank you, Julia Seay, for being such a great advocate for mental health and for adding your important words of wisdom to this work. I may be biased, but I believe that one of my favorite "Westlake daughters" is a rising star in this world.

Writing a book like this requires having people to keep you honest. I truly appreciate the reviews and expertise provided by Chantrise Holliman, Jenelle Wingfield, and Dawn Perry. Thank you for your feedback, wonderful ladies. Also, to my editor—David Ferris. You truly made this flow better without changing my voice.

Finally, I must acknowledge the love of my life, Dedra Woolfolk. You are my motivator, confidante, moral support, and heartbeat. I love you more each and every day we are together. Thank you for all of your input into this book, from the years we spent raising our boys to the daily grind of putting our words to paper.

Foreword

In a world where a college degree has basically become a professional prerequisite, experienced adults understand the need to assist young people in reaching their scholastic goals. But while many have only a vague idea of what this assistance must consist of, I can personally attest to one thing for sure—Geary Woolfolk is one of the people who has genuinely dedicated himself to the challenge of helping college-bound teenagers construct individual paths to prepare for their undergraduate years, and his direction has yielded legitimate benefits for the young people that he has worked with. I should know—as his eldest son, very few people are more qualified than me to give a personal and honest review of his methods and his genuine desire to help the new generation of young people succeed. I know that my dad has a workable and useful model for genuine college readiness; I have experienced it, I have seen it in action, and I am excited for him to share it with more teenagers in our community and beyond.

Geary Woolfolk's guidance has produced very real results in several aspects of my own life, and the impact that he has had in the academic and college prep realms has been among the most notable examples. From a young age, my dad made it clear to my two brothers and me that we were fully expected to fund our college educations through our own merit. This initially seemed like a daunting task and an unreasonable prospect, and without the proper preparation and information, it would have been. However, my dad had full confidence that he could lay the necessary groundwork by assisting us with developing a viable plan of action, and that it was simply up to us to discover our personal motivations and dedicate ourselves to the hard work. He knew what we were capable of, and he knew what we could accomplish with the proper guidance. In the end, his intentions ultimately came to fruition. The strategies detailed in the pages of this book related to goal setting, extracurricular planning, immersive reading, standardized test prep, and much more were indispensable factors that have allowed me and my siblings to gain admission to the universities we were interested in, earn full-ride academic scholarships, and thrive in our undergraduate studies. I am overwhelmingly convinced that my dad's counsel can help to vastly improve any college-bound high schooler's odds of success.

But to truly help the younger generation, it takes more than possessing great advice and having the general ability to communicate it. It also requires a true sense of responsibility, a sincere desire to see young people succeed, and an ability to connect with the high school age group. I can personally attest to the fact that Geary Woolfolk is passionate about supporting the teenagers in our community. For my entire life, I have watched my dad mentor numerous groups of teens at our church, including chaperoning several convention and mission trips and leading a Sunday morning worship service catered to the needs and experiences of high schoolers. I have observed him encouraging teens that he knows by attending their performances and sporting events, and I have seen him travel out of the state for such competitions when necessary. This support does not simply consist of attendance; on occasion, he has even volunteered to capture their best moments as an amateur cameraman.

Moreover, there are few things that frustrate him more than seeing capable members of upcoming generations fail to reach their full capabilities not due to a lack of ability, but due to a lack of access to information. I know from firsthand experience that Geary Woolfolk derives genuine joy from helping high school kids reach their potential, and that the teenagers who have trusted him and been open to his recommendations have found themselves in better positions and value him for it. My dad has been actively involved at my alma mater high school for years, serving as president of the magnet program's booster club, a leader in the School Governance Council, and a dedicated volunteer. He has worked to establish his own scholarship program for students, been trusted to chaperone multiple international school trips, and has "adopted" several students as his "school sons and daughters." He has helped many of these teens with admissions and scholarship applications, summer program searches, and interview preparation for prestigious programs (such as the Georgia Governor's Honors Program). My dad has demonstrated time and time again that helping the upcoming generation has deep meaning and a very important place in his life, and that he is consistently willing to offer up his time and effort to help and support young people. To me, this long-term commitment highlights the fact that he truly has this generation's best interests at heart. I hope that it encourages others to trust his college readiness guidance in the way that I have; I certainly have not been disappointed.

–Christopher Woolfolk

Before We Get Started

Our Story

My wife, Dr. Dedra Woolfolk, and I worked together to place our sons in the best position for success. She is the Dean of the College of Arts and Sciences at Point University and a Professor of Biological Sciences. We have been married for twenty-nine wonderful years while living in the Atlanta metropolitan area. We are true partners in all facets of life, especially when raising our children. During their years in elementary school, Dedra was a PTA mom and parent volunteer extraordinaire. She demonstrated to our boys how hard work and discipline leads to achieving success. Her perspective as a mom, and especially as a college dean, has been instrumental in helping me write this book.

We raised our sons to be academically solid and strong college candidates by fostering a culture of excellence and a mindset of greatness. Starting in middle school, they were told these three truths:

1. You have three months from the time you graduate high school to leave our house.
2. You are going to college.
3. Neither you nor I are paying for it.

I know these statements can seem pretty severe, but the responsibility did not lie with them, as my wife and I let them know we would be partnering on this endeavor for a debt-free college education. Therefore, I had to figure out a plan that would greatly increase our chances for success and implement it without applying undue stress on my boys.

The goal of not paying the full cost of college tuition is a real concern:

- » The rising cost of college continues to outpace inflation.
- » According to *Forbes*, "the price of college increased almost eight times faster than wages."
- » The state of student loan debt in the United States is alarming.
- » Total student loan debt: $1.56 trillion
- » Total U.S. borrowers with student loan debt: $44.7 million
- » Student loan delinquency or default rate: 11.4% (90+ days delinquent)

You do not want to sacrifice the quality of education due to the cost of tuition. Recognizing these concerns highlights the importance of planning.

I developed a plan for my eldest when he was in middle school, and we worked together to reach our goal of a debt-free college education. The summer after his junior year of high school, we started researching potential colleges and then set out on our first college tour. When we returned, I learned that the college admissions process had completely changed since I applied to college. Turns out I was planning for a goal without first understanding what colleges were now looking for. Thankfully, we had incorporated some of the most important components needed to secure a few great scholarships, and I had four years to create a new plan for the next two children.

As a result of planning and execution by each of my sons, all three of my boys were able to secure multiple major scholarships offered by colleges and universities:

- » Christopher, my eldest, had several acceptances including full academic scholarships to Mississippi State University and Howard University, but decided to attend the University of Kentucky on a full academic scholarship. As I am writing this book, he has just graduated from The University of Texas School of Law (#14 national ranking at time of acceptance) on a scholarship that covered roughly 2/3 of his tuition. It is important to note that in high school he became a National Achievement Merit Finalist, which is based off his *PSAT performance.*
- » Brian, my middle son, is currently enrolled at The University of Georgia on a full academic (plus) scholarship that included a summer study abroad at the University of Oxford as well as afforded him a spring break educational trip to Bali, Indonesia. Among his college choices were acceptances to Cornell, Vanderbilt, University of Virginia, Washington University in St Louis, (waitlisted at Yale), and tuition scholarships to Rice University and the University of Southern California. It is also important to note that he was the *STAR Student* of his graduating class, a title awarded to the student with the highest SAT score in their graduating class (requires a top 10% ranking).
- » Aaron, affectionately known as Baby Boy, recently graduated high school and decided to take his talent to Clemson University. He is a part of their prestigious National Scholars Program that covers the full cost of attending college (including books, travel, laptop, etc.). They spend their first summer traveling in South Africa followed by a study abroad summer session in Cape Town. Among his college choices were top merit scholarship awards to Vanderbilt University, University of North Carolina at Chapel Hill, North Carolina A&T State University; tuition scholarships to Georgia Institute of Technology, Auburn University and University of Georgia; acceptances to Cornell, University of

Virginia, Washington University in St Louis, Johns Hopkins, Northwestern, and Harvey Mudd. He graduated from high school as valedictorian and *STAR Student.*

A major contributing factor to their scholarship accumulation was their performance on either the PSAT, SAT, or ACT college entrance exams. Preparing for these tests was a large part of our college prep planning, so the benefits of their stellar performances were intentional. I also want to point out their experiences while in college. Christopher graduated undergrad magna cum laude, the vast majority of Brian's grades have been As going into his senior year of college pursuing a double major in Advertising and Computer Science, and Aaron just completed his freshman year with all As. I am very proud of my sons because no matter how much I planned, they had to want and work for these achievements for themselves.

I bring their accomplishments to your attention for the following reasons:

- » Proper planning produces results
- » Discipline is important for carrying out your plan
- » Outstanding ACT/SAT scores can put you in the conversation for great opportunities
- » Success looks different for every student

Their success is a direct result of how much they invested in themselves to reach their college goals. I am writing this book because I believe that if you choose to invest in yourself, you will reach your dreams as well!

Special Note: To learn more about me and my wife along with what drives my passion for teens, you can visit *woolfolkworks.com/biography.*

Message to Parents

The goal of this book is to provide your child with as many college options as possible. Before I press onwards, there are a few thoughts that you, as a parent, should consider as you read through this material.

1. **Dream Big**—*Shoot for the stars, because even if you come up short, the moon and the planets are still out of this world!*

    One of the reasons why many kids do not fully realize their potential is because adults in their lives have set limits well below their ability. **Do not constrain your child from achieving their full potential**. You should not only let them dream big but encourage them to do so! However, be aware that there is a delicate balance when it comes to setting expectations. Set them too low and they will never be challenged to surpass them and discover new abilities; set them too high and they may consider themselves a failure and become discouraged and depressed. Take the time to truly understand your child's abilities and always set expectations just high enough to challenge them. Encourage them to achieve success while avoiding any discouragement when they come up short.

2. **It is THEIR Dream**—*Do not shape your kid's future in your own image or limit their options based on your own experiences.*

    I have witnessed children handcuffed to a parent's desires or limitations way too often. You believe there is a certain college experience that will be best for your child, and I commend you for wanting the best for them. As you and your child work together to plan for their future, please keep the following in mind:

    › Your ideals are just that—yours. Is your goal to raise a clone or an independent thinker? Guide them but allow them to forge their own path.

> Until you and your child have had the opportunity to thoroughly investigate and (hopefully) unbiasedly visit a variety of college campuses, it is really not possible to determine the sort of college that will work best for them.
> Most importantly, it is ***not*** about what you want but about what they need!

Special Note: If you attended college and your experience was great, you will want the same for your child, I get it. While the college you attended may have served you well, that was a while ago and the college landscape has greatly changed!

3. **Achieving the Dream**—*Most kids need someone to believe in them until they can believe in themselves.*

    Christopher, my oldest, decided he wanted to attend law school, but since I thought his choices were too "safe," I encouraged him to apply to a few top-20 nationally ranked schools. He was accepted to Georgetown and The University of Texas at Austin, and even though he knew that attending one of these law schools would put him in the best position after graduation, he was a bit reluctant to compete against some of the best minds in the country. After successfully completing his first semester, he began to believe that he would graduate. After the first semester of his second year, he knew he was good enough to graduate from the fourteenth-ranked law school in the country.

    But why would anyone enroll in a school without fully believing that they could graduate? Christopher attributes one of our heart-to-heart talks as his motivation to move forward: the conversation where I told him that I had no doubt that he was good enough to do it. My point is that *many people underachieve simply because, without anyone to believe in them, they do not believe that they can achieve success.*

As you continue to read, I encourage you to carry this mindset with you:

» Dream big with no predetermined limits. Any restrictions will come naturally as the student progresses through high school, as college acceptances come in, and as financial decisions are made.
» Instead of imposing your will on your student, help them find their fit.
» Always encourage your child to push through. Do not belittle them for coming up short but encourage them to learn from the experience and congratulate them for their effort.

Final Notes

I have worked with many families through seminars and personal coaching and typically explain all the principles, techniques, lessons, and steps to *parents*. However, I chose to address this book to you, *students*, because no matter how badly a parent wants their child to achieve success, you *must* want *it* for yourself. Your future goals, dreams, and whatever steps you must take to reach that point in your life are your "it." As the journey will be difficult to attempt on your own, I do not just highly recommend but insist that your parent (or another adult family member or friend that is invested in your future) read this book in its entirety along with you so that you will have a support system.

Here are some notes to consider before reading this book:

» This book is based on the experience of my family, including lessons learned from mistakes we made plus additional research on things we may have missed. In addition, I have drawn from the experience I have gained from working with students within my community.

- » My goal is to place you in the most competitive position to fill out your college applications. I want to make sure you have the most outstanding high school resumé in order to present the best application possible.
- » Understand now that once you hit your senior year, applying to college can seem like a part-time job. You will absolutely thank yourself for planning ahead.
- » There are goals and objectives listed at the start of each grade-level chapter. I encourage you to use them as a checklist to refer to as you progress through each year of high school.
- » You may run across sections you feel confident that you already have a handle on. I encourage you to read them anyway to make sure you understand why the information is important for becoming a strong college-bound student.
- » *It is important for me to state that while we were very successful implementing our plan(s), our journey started with prayer and was executed based on our relationship with God.*
- » Ultimately, the end goal is to build the best college resumé for any college-minded high school student. There is no single ideal college application profile as each one must be unique to the individual student.

In order to get the maximum value out of this book, you must make the commitment to perform up to your potential in the classroom. While I do provide tips that will make you a stronger high school student, I primarily focus on the things you will need to concentrate on outside of the classroom. When it comes to college admission decisions, your effort in and outside of the classroom will work hand-in-hand to make you a strong applicant.

Planning for Success

The Guide

Imagine any city that you want to visit, whether in the United States or abroad. Here are four options for how to visit the sights of this city: no itinerary, a self-guided tour, an all-inclusive tour, or the use of a travel agent.

No itinerary is for the traveler that likes to just figure it out as they go along. This approach may have more flexibility, but you will waste time if you are scrambling to find transportation, have no idea of the hours sites are open, run out of money, or show up to places that are sold out on the day you are there. This will likely result in missing out on attractions or simply running out of time.

A self-guided tour requires you to do a lot of research on the best places to visit, the hours different places are open, the best transportation between sites, and locations to eat along the way, and then you have to organize a schedule to fit everything in. Putting together this trip takes *a lot* of time, but this effort ensures that you make the most of your visit. However, it omits any spots that are hidden gems known only by the locals.

All-inclusive tours have two significant advantages over self-guided tours. First, they require very little work because everything will be planned for you. Second, you will be provided with a local guide that will enhance your trip by providing you with local knowledge and transportation so all you have to do is show up and enjoy your visit. The downside is that the cost for such a trip will be much higher than any other option, and you will not be able to tailor the agenda to exactly what you want to see.

Using a travel agent is the best way to reap many of the benefits of an all-inclusive tour, yet greatly reduce the time investment of a self-guided tour. A travel agent has experience putting together trips all over the world, so they know how to properly plan for yours. Instead of doing all the research on your own, your agent will guide you through decisions as you work together to plan your itinerary and make sure you have the required documents and finances. They will reduce the likelihood of missing out on a great attraction and can find you a guide that has local knowledge. You get the full experience without an enormous amount of research and a large price tag. Best of all, you get an experience specifically customized for you.

For high school students, to be accepted to their dream college is just like a desire to visit a dream city. My concern is that too many students traverse through high school with no itinerary and are not exposed to the requirements of college applications until they become seniors. At that point, many options will not be available because of the lack of research conducted ahead of time. Some students prepare for the college application season by doing well in classes and studying for the ACT/SAT, but they wait too long to determine what colleges are looking for in applicants. These students' only hope is that they happened to meet the requirements.

It would be awesome if there was an all-inclusive college application service that does all of the prep work for you, earns As in all of your classes, aces the ACT/SAT for you, starts a successful international non-profit organization in your name, and gets you into Stanford. Sadly, even if this service existed, most of us would never be able to afford it.

Just as it takes a lot of knowledge and expertise to build an ideal itinerary for a dream trip, it takes a lot of research and experience of the college application process to make an effective plan for your dream college. Similar to a travel agent helping a client create an itinerary, my goal is to greatly reduce the time you spend seeking information and guide you in crafting your college plan. The purpose of this book is to be a ***model*** for you to build a plan to achieve your ideal college application profile with enough time for you to have the required elements for your application. This book is a ***guide*** designed to place you in the best possible position to receive your *ideal college acceptances* based on your unique profile, to demonstrate the various ways to build an *attractive college and scholarship application profile*, and to help build a *college-ready student*, all while navigating your four years in high school.

If you are:

- » A middle school student—reading this book will give you a great head start on your high school career by allowing you to start planning for success early.
- » A student in ninth or tenth grade—you are in the perfect position to actively work through this book as you progress through high school.
- » An upperclassman in high school—use this book as a guide for navigating through the college application process and as a resource for tips on being ready for success in college.

No matter the grade you are currently in, *I strongly suggest* **reading the book in its entirety first and then referring back to it as a guide while you navigate high school.**

My dream after high school was to attend Brown University, where I received a full tuition scholarship. I was also accepted to all three military academies (West Point, Naval, and Air Force), and I chose to enroll in the Air Force Academy because it was prestigious and people in my life pushed me to attend. While it was a great experience for a year, it was just not a good fit for me. Since I excelled in math and physics in high school, I was advised to major in engineering in college. So, after the Academy, I enrolled at The Georgia Institute of Technology (GT) for engineering, but I honestly had no idea what an engineer was. Although I was not able to succeed academically at GT, I eventually found success at Georgia State University where I earned a BS in Mathematics. My six-year-long, tough road to a degree taught me valuable lessons that I passed on to my children and will now share with you:

» Find the path that best suits *you* and do not allow others to dictate your path.
» Understand the value of taking over ownership of your future.
» Fortify yourself with information in order to make educated decisions along your journey.
» *Become a college-ready student, not just a student that can get into college, so that you will be ready to conquer the challenges that you will face at the next level.*

The Wheels

I have witnessed too many high school seniors who intend on going to college but have no idea what colleges are looking for in an applicant. I have listened to too many parents lamenting over their children not being competitive enough for exclusive schools and big scholarships. Waiting until late junior or early senior year of high school to understand what it takes to be an ideal candidate on a college application will be too late to plan for becoming one. However, if you are starting this book as a junior or senior, there are still steps you can take to make yourself a more attractive candidate.

Over the span of three children and ten years, I have figured out how a student can become a strong college applicant. However, our family spent too much time researching information that others have found before me. When creating the metaphorical vehicle that will carry you to college, **my goal is to prevent families from having to "reinvent the wheel"** by providing a model for you to use as you build yours. ***Remember: This book is designed to be your guide to building a student profile that is attractive to college admissions and that provides you with as many college options as possible***.

Beginning your college planning late in your high school career is like developing only one wheel and then attempting to ride a unicycle all the way to college. Therefore, I am providing you with a model for becoming a strong college applicant through a full four years of preparation. By helping you build one "wheel" per year, you will understand the steps you should be taking at each level of high school.

Getting into college is an important step towards your future, but it is not your final destination. So, along the way, I will be providing you with additional knowledge to develop your skills as a learner and your college readiness. This is **the car** that you will build on top of the wheels (your high school foundation) to drive off to college and beyond. These skills will not only help you get into college; they will ensure that you successfully complete college within four years while equipped with the basic tools necessary to navigate all the way to the future of your dreams.

For each grade level in high school, I will provide knowledge, explain concepts, assign tasks, and guide you with your goal setting. This will all be essential for constructing your wheels and assembling your car, i.e., becoming a strong, college-ready applicant. I will identify the type of milestones you should be aiming for, when they should be done, and the importance of each task.

I will supply the general framework needed for any student to be successful in the admissions process and in college, but the specific "whats" and "hows" will be unique to your situation. It is up to you to choose the way you will fulfill these requirements based on your situation, strengths, and opportunities. At the end of the day, the wheels for each student will not be the same size, and every car will be distinct. But it is much more advantageous to enter the race with four good tires built over the four years of high school than to compete with deflated ones because you did not properly prepare for college.

The Plan

The American College Testing (ACT) and Scholastic Aptitude/Assessment Test (SAT) are the two major standardized tests required for admission to most colleges. They were once competency exams designed to measure how much content a student mastered in high school. Nowadays, the ACT/SAT tests how well you have prepared for the test itself. Naturally, the advantage goes to those who have the benefit of foresight and prep materials. The college application is now beginning to move in the same direction. The application was designed to represent the results of a student's high school career, but now college application prep is needed to be competitive. This requires properly setting **goals**, understanding the **requirements**, and creating a **roadmap** to satisfy them: deciding which type of college to aim for, knowing what these schools want to see on an application, and having a plan to fulfill them.

Goals

Without exploring the opportunities that exist for college choices, your goals will be shortsighted, and you may limit your options for college. You must first answer the question: "What are you working towards?"

Looking ahead to your senior year, there are three levels every college-bound student should strive to aim for regarding college applications: "safe schools," "target schools," and "stretch schools." There is no set definition for which schools should go into each category. Every student will have their own set of criteria based upon their preferences and individual abilities. The general understanding for each level is as follows:

» **Safe school**—A college you feel 95% certain that you can get into and is a clear financial fit. This may not be your top choice, but it satisfies your requirements for higher education.
» **Target school**—A college you have a decent chance to get into with a potential financial fit. This is a school you prefer to attend and has benefits that extend beyond meeting your minimum requirements.
» **Stretch school**—A college where you have a lower chance of gaining acceptance, but it can provide an added bonus if you are able to attend.

Special Note: After doing your homework on schools, I recommend applying to roughly three schools per level (potentially a few more target schools) and only applying to schools you are willing and able to attend (I will give strategies for finding and narrowing down colleges later).

Following the guidance of this book, I want you to have the following by April of your senior year:

» An acceptance letter to at least one of your stretch schools.
» An acceptance letter to each of your target schools along with a hopeful scholarship to one.
» Acceptance and scholarship offers to most of your safe schools.

> *Remember: making yourself a better candidate for college admissions also makes you a better candidate for receiving scholarship money from colleges.*

As you make your way through high school and begin researching majors and colleges, you may begin to discover what you consider to be your dream school(s). I define a ***dream* school** as a specific college that you have your heart set on attending, a type of college that you feel you must attend, or a college you will definitely attend if accepted. *Your* dream college should not be based on the general consensus, and it may not even be on your "stretch school" list. At any point throughout your high school journey, your dream school(s) may change as you learn more about yourself and your life goals.

I have found that many families believe that prestigious colleges are financially out of reach, and so they do not consider creating plans to qualify for one. Many of the top-rated private schools in the country offer financial packages that allow for students to attend at ***no cost*** with family incomes less than $65,000, and have very reasonable rates for incomes under $150,000. It is important to understand the affordability of these schools as early as possible in order to create a plan to gain acceptance.

I know that only a small percentage of students will be aiming for the most prestigious schools, but according to Kaitlin Mulhere's 2019 YahooMoney article, there are 75 colleges that "will offer admitted students enough financial aid to cover the difference between a college's price of attendance and a family's ability to pay" and "some colleges take the promise one step further and meet need without requiring students or their parents to take out loans." Not all programs are as generous as the numbers I just provided, but knowing that these programs exist should serve as motivation to fully research the available college options. (I will have more to say on this topic later.)

Requirements

Without knowing what it takes to obtain your goal, it is impossible to build a detailed plan to achieve it. Next, you need to answer the second question: "What steps are required to fulfill your goal(s)?"

Colleges ask a range of questions in an attempt to determine which students will succeed at their school. Most students convey an unsystematic high school career on their application. The risk, even for great students, is that this will result in an unexceptional application and leave them wondering how they missed out on attending their dream college. Submitting a respectable Grade Point Average (GPA) along with participating in some extracurricular activities at school is not enough to build a strong college application. **I will guide you on how to be more purposeful in your actions during your high school career so that your application will stand out!**

I do not expect many freshmen to have locked down the specific schools that will go into their college application pool. As a matter of fact, I discourage being *too* focused on specific colleges this early in your high school career. I believe your high school journey will help dictate the schools that are the best fit for you. What I *do* encourage is opening up to as many possibilities as imaginable. This means:

» Learning about the many types of colleges that exist.
» Not allowing your pool of potential colleges to be narrowed down simply because you did not understand what the schools require of their candidates.
» Taking the necessary steps to be a strong candidate for whatever colleges you may want to qualify for in the future.

You can do a quick internet search on "What are colleges looking for?" and you will find plenty of sites that list—a good GPA, challenging coursework, extracurriculars, volunteer work, test scores, essay, leadership, etc. My role is to guide you to properly meeting the requirements for any college you eventually plan to submit an application to and explain what is important, why it is important, and how to set milestones to meet your goals.

Roadmap

Without having a plan to satisfy the requirements for your goals, you are simply wishing for your dreams to come true. Finally, you must answer: "How do I build a plan that will give me the maximum number of college options?"

Imagine a family residing in Richmond, Virginia sending their 18-year-old (licensed) child on a road trip to Disneyland in California. To give their child the best chance to make it to their destination, the parents have saved up enough money for a hotel, food, and entertainment for the child's stay in California. They even provided their child with a well-maintained and reliable car for the road trip. After the goodbyes, the child starts the journey to their destination—no map, no GPS, no directions—only with the name of their destination and the knowledge that California is somewhere west.

You and your family want to ensure that you can get to your next destination—college. Your parent(s) likely had a desire to find the best possible primary and secondary schools to prepare you for college and may have even considered the cost of tuition before you started high school. It is better to NOT leave it to chance that you will take the correct path to your destination. This is the point where you need a map or GPS to provide you with directions; *you need a plan!*

Early in the next chapter, I will provide you with an outline for goal setting and building effective plans, but I also encourage you to find other resources as well. At this point I wish to emphasize that:

» A plan must be written down or it will never be properly executed.

- » A plan must be alive: it should be reviewed often and adjusted as necessary.
- » Another person's plan can never serve as your own, but it can be adopted and tailored to fit your situation.

In addition to becoming a strong college applicant, it is just as important to become a college-ready student. Four-year college graduation rates are alarmingly low. A notable contributing factor is that high schools are preparing students to have the scholastic foundation to get into college but do not teach students how to successfully navigate higher education. Few students have the ability to naturally adapt and avoid the pitfalls that await them at the next level. **I will help your plan incorporate how to become a student who will be ready to succeed when you walk onto your future college campus.**

The Execution (Keys to Success)

Creating and sticking to a plan is no easy task, and knowing what to do and having the fortitude to do it are two completely different animals. Staying focused for the four years of high school is a lot to ask. This is why I believe the following **three keys to success** are critical for your journey.

#1 The most powerful question in the universe is "Why?"

When it comes to education, when it comes to learning, and when it comes to your growth, the strongest tool you have at your disposal is the question, "Why?" Asking "Why" is the key to effective studying as well as the key to learning analytical and critical thinking skills. Asking "Why" is the key to becoming an independent thinker! If you have not already adopted this mindset, it is to your advantage to start now.

I have shared my experiences and advice with parents in my local community for the last few years through speaking engagements and seminars. I have also provided a two-page outline of action items and strategies for the parents who were unable to attend my talks. When I run into parents who attended my presentations, they excitedly tell me how much they appreciate the experiences I shared with them. Contrastingly, I typically do not hear much feedback from families who read the handouts without hearing me speak. The problem is that without understanding the *whys* behind the advice I give, it is difficult for them to appreciate and recognize their importance. Therefore, my goal in this book is to not only provide you with *what* you should be doing, but to also explain the *why* behind the concepts.

Whether it is with respect to learning or life in general, **the *why* provides the value, the value encourages the buy-in, the buy-in prompts the plan, and the plan is your path to success.**

#2 The most powerful factor for success is "Grit"

One of the best Ted Talks I have ever watched is "Grit: The Power of Passion and Perseverance" by Angela Lee Duckworth. I highly recommend watching this video before continuing this book. Seriously, stop reading, go to YouTube, and watch this video now. I will wait…

Simply stated from my perspective: when comparing one student with great aptitude, a super high SAT score, and a perfect GPA to another student with good grades, a decent SAT score, and a lot of "Grit," I will place my money on the second student every time. Grit is that magic ingredient that overcomes conventional wisdom regarding what it takes to be successful. A homeless man could never wind up owning the largest movie studio in the world without grit (just think of Tyler Perry). An athlete could not go from being cut off his high school basketball team to becoming the greatest player to ever grace the court of the NBA without grit (Michael Jordan). A sexually abused girl born into poverty in the rural town of Kosciusko, Mississippi could not go on to become a billionaire media executive and philanthropist without grit (Oprah Winfrey).

Doing well in school and in life depends on much more than your ability to learn quickly. Instilling this mindset brings so much value into the journey you are about to embark on. Grit helps level the playing field for ALL students. It gives hope to the student that is not in contention for valedictorian or the top 1% of their class. Grit cultivates greatness while removing the stress of the need for perfection. **Grit promotes a mindset of growth where your effort constantly pushes what you believe to be the limits of your ability and overcomes any obstacle placed in your path.**

#3 The most powerful quality needed for college is "Discipline"

One of the most important characteristics needed to be successful in college—well, in many areas throughout life—is *discipline*. **The lack of discipline has cost students millions of dollars through lost tuition, has resulted in semesters wasted, and has even brought about the onset of depression.** Understanding these realities now gives you adequate time to be ready for your eventual first day of college. Developing your discipline in preparation for that day will also greatly benefit you while in high school. Let's delve into what I mean by discipline and talk about the key elements of discipline to focus on developing while in high school.

There are two kinds of discipline: one is external and the other is internal. Acting in accordance with the regulations of a home, group, or society is considered "external discipline." We are motivated to adhere to these rules by punishments or negative consequences that are enforced by the regulating authorities. "Internal discipline" is different in that we have to find our own motivation for adhering to guidelines, because these guidelines are based on the expectations that we set for ourselves. Negative consequences still exist, but wisdom is found in recognizing the benefits of adhering to self-discipline. While both are an important part of everyone's lives, as a student, developing internal discipline is what leads to success in school and in life.

I have formulated five elements designed to build and strengthen discipline in your life. We will focus on developing these "Elements of Discipline" over the span of high school in preparation for becoming a well-disciplined, college-ready student.

1. **Organization** leads to higher grades, less frustration, improved self-esteem, completing more tasks, and submitting better quality work.
2. **Motivation** at high levels increases persistence, enhances cognitive processes, and leads to improved performance in school.
3. **Perseverance** is a trait of students who understand the value of hard work, hone their problem-solving skills, and take responsibility for their own academic progress—*grit in action*! They do not make excuses or blame others for failure.
4. **Consistency** ensures that students do not fall behind and that their grades will truly reflect their ability in the classroom.
5. **Time management** helps students get more organized, build a good reputation, become more focused, and most importantly, have more time for a social life!

Integrating all of your keys to success reinvents your potential as a student and beyond:

» Asking *why* will make you a much more successful **learner.**
» Having *grit* will instill the determination to be an **overcomer** of any setbacks or obstacles along your way.
» Establishing self-*discipline* will make you a successful **executor** of your plan.

Internalizing these keys will assure that you drive off to success!

Ninth Grade—Buying In

You must be invested in your own education!

"An investment in knowledge pays the best interest."
–Benjamin Franklin

Your freshman year of high school brings about new beginnings. You have the opportunity to redefine yourself and become the type of person you want to be for the next four years. You should build on your known strengths, strive to mature as a student, and most importantly, explore exciting possibilities outside of your comfort zone. I want you to be thrilled about defining the new and improved YOU!

Again, the goal of this book is to provide you with knowledge you need to "drive off" towards college success. These are our goals/objectives that will make up the freshman year wheel of your car:

- » Understand the importance of **reading regularly** and **ACT/SAT prep**
- » Instill the importance of establishing **ownership** of the future
- » Establish a successful attitude by learning a **mindset of excellence** and why **everything you do matters**
- » Recognize the importance of managing **mental health**
- » Incorporate the first three elements of good **discipline: motivation, focus on time management, and focus on organization**

» Perform action items towards building your ideal college admissions profile:
   › Start your ACT/SAT prep
   › Explore extracurricular activities
   › Create a logging document to track your activities, programs, awards, and honors
   › Assess the start of your freshman year to stay on track
   › Research programs and activities for the upcoming summer
   › Learn the proper way to work towards your future college major
   › Develop your essay writing skills
   › Begin your college research
   › Create an email account used for college interest

Freshman Focus Point: Lack of motivation tends to come from lack of purpose, planning or passion. Without seeing the purpose or value in what you are doing, it is hard to stay motivated. If you have purpose but no written plan with measurable goals, it is easy to get disheartened about the reality of meeting those goals. Having a purpose with a plan is essential but may not be enough if you are not passionate about what you are doing. While it would be ideal to be passionate about every step in the process of achieving your goal, this may not always be the case. When working towards your goal, there may be times when you are not really invested in what you are currently doing. In these times, you must focus on the passion you have for your ultimate goal.

I want you to take a moment and dream a bit about the path to your future as you come up with answers to the following questions (I will refer back to these in a couple of sections):

1. What are a few awards and honors you want to have at your high school graduation?

2. What is the dream college you want to attend?
3. Do you want to attend graduate or professional school?
4. What do you want to do as your dream job after college?
5. What positions or roles do you want to have in your career?
6. Where do you want your dream home to be located?
7. What do you want your future family to look like, either by companionship or a family defined by friends?

Now ask yourself if simply ***wanting*** to achieve your ideal future is enough to obtain these dreams. If you truly want what you consider to be your ideal future, are you willing to invest in yourself to achieve it? Are you willing to work towards your dreams through any obstacles? **The bridge between where you are now and living that dream is dependent on you, not your parent.**

This is the same mindset that needs to be applied to actions that affect your future. Therefore, I encourage you to take ownership of your own life and your future. You can do this without feeling like you must be perfect or putting undue pressure on yourself. There is no exact route to take because your path will be unique to you, and it will adjust as you take actions to put yourself in the best possible position for success.

Do not beat yourself up for your shortcomings. Do not think of yourself as a failure when you fall short. Celebrate the positives and enjoy your wins. *Parents: this message is just as much for you as it is for your child.*

Before The Application

The Fundamentals—Laying the Groundwork

It is very important to establish two essential components if you want to be a successful college-bound student: reading comprehension and ACT/SAT prep.

Reading for Fun

My wife, Dedra, began reading books to our oldest son at an early age. Once he was able to read on his own, he could be found working his way through two to three books at a time. His younger brothers followed in his footsteps; they always seemed to have a book in their hands. Ultimately, this had a positive impact on their success in high school and strengthened their testing abilities.

As Patrick Sullivan pointed it out in his open letter to high school students published in the May-June 2006 issue of *Academe*:

> *"The value of reading as preparation for college should never be underestimated, not even as the focus of higher education turns to STEM majors and career preparation."* He goes on to say, *"…that reading for pleasure produces important benefits across a variety of academic disciplines (including math) and that 'reading is actually linked to increased cognitive progress over time.' Obviously, these cognitive gains will help you regardless of your major or career aspirations."*

Hopefully, you already enjoy reading. If not, you should do your best to get to a point where you do. Reading is the foundation for knowledge, education, learning, thinking, writing, and the list goes on. The above quote supports my theory that a deficiency in reading comprehension is the reason why students who are otherwise capable struggle in school and perform poorly on standardized tests. The ability to read textbooks and assignments with complete understanding is a necessary precept for learning. The struggle with standardized testing is not always due to the inability to demonstrate a mastery of content, but the inability to quickly comprehend the question itself.

My high school English teachers will be in total shock if they ever read this, but when your teacher gives a reading assignment, please *do the reading*. I struggled throughout my life due to poor reading comprehension and writing skills, yet here I am authoring a book that preaches the value of reading!

Think of reading as the oil in your car. Have you ever heard of a "well-oiled machine"? Engine oil has several vital purposes, all designed to keep the engine running smoothly. Bad oil will cause the engine to run sluggish or even burn completely out. The engine to your car is the plan you are building to your future. Your plan will include many of your goals in life, and reading comprehension skills are needed to accomplish every aspect of those goals. Just like bad oil, bad reading comprehension skills will cause your plans to run sluggish.

If you simply do not like to read, and I say this in love, **get over it**! You may not be happy about it, but reading is something you simply must do. Consider developing a support system that will keep you accountable and motivate you to read. For example, find a reading buddy or join a book club. If you do not have a book club in your community or school, start one. Taking this initiative will serve another purpose that you will soon learn more about.

If you are not reading regularly, it is never too late to get started. Frequent reading is a must. Just like building a muscle, you must constantly exercise your reading skills to strengthen them. It does not matter what you are reading as long as you are reading something. You will be assigned enough educational material to read at school, so I suggest recreational reading just for fun. Picking a good fictional series will keep you reading beyond one book. I strongly encourage you to check out the Helen Ruffin Reading Bowl Booklist and follow Project Lit on social media for age-appropriate book ideas.

In my household, screen time (video games, streaming sites, social media, etc.) was never allowed Monday through Thursday during the school year, which provided my boys a great opportunity to read. I would often ask them questions about what they were reading, what they thought about a character, and what they thought might happen next. This way, they were comprehending and analyzing as they read. Exercising their "reading muscles" has served each of my sons well in their educational pursuits.

Special Note: While limited screen time worked for us, I do not necessarily recommend the same approach, as every family dynamic is different. However, I must recommend that *you* set your own limit on screen time during the school week to eliminate distractions and make school and extracurricular activities the priority. I especially suggest placing a hard limit on time spent on social media. According to studies referenced in articles like "How Using Social Media Affects Teenagers" found on *childmind.org*, social media leads to "increased feelings of depression, anxiety, poor body image and loneliness," as well as diminishes writing and communication skills. *Addictioncenter.com* states that "social media addiction is a behavioral addiction that ... impairs other important life areas." Placing restrictions on yourself will allow you to remain in control of social media and not allow it to control you.

When my middle son Brian went off to college, his freedom to play video games, watch videos, and stream content any time he wanted to distracted him from effectively managing his time. He eventually needed to apply similar guidelines as the ones he had at home. You may want to use his strategy of installing a web browser plug-in that limits the usage of any identified website to an hour each weekday. Christopher, my oldest, can spend a good deal of time on Twitter, but while in college and law school, he would completely remove the app from his phone for weeks during important periods that required his undivided attention. This is how you, too, can stay in control of social media.

Reading Challenge

Now that I have addressed the primary obstacles for having the time to read, I want you to take the **Commitment to Reading Challenge** over the next year: for example, challenge yourself to read one book per month or read for at least two hours per week. Pick the option that best fits you.

I *will* read a minimum of _____ books over the next year.

–OR–

I *will* read a minimum of _____ hours per week over the next year.

ACT/SAT Prep

One of the biggest misconceptions about the college admissions process is the idea of a holistic application. With colleges putting more focus on components like extracurricular activities and community involvement, many families have started to interpret this to mean test scores and Grade Point Average (GPA) will no longer be the critical factors in determining college acceptance. Colleges will indeed consider the entire student profile, but *test scores matter*! Scores on college entrance exams can make an application "pop," providing the student with a competitive advantage over other applicants. When other aspects of the application are equivalent, the deciding factor will likely be the ACT/SAT score, especially when the conversation shifts from acceptances to scholarships. While it is true that test scores alone will not bring in the money, without them, being competitive is an uphill battle.

If you choose to target a prestigious college or university, know that you will be competing against other applicants who all have high class rankings and impressive ACT/SAT scores. Not performing well on these tests may keep you from being considered for admittance. As you build the four wheels of each year in high school, your car will not be able to move until you place tires on those wheels. Your ACT/SAT scores are these tires, and the better the condition of your tires, the farther you can travel. If you do everything in this book but you do not prepare for the ACT/SAT properly, your car may get you to a college, but your tires may not get you all the way to your dream school.

So, let me share with you some tips I used with my boys to help them achieve excellent scores:

» Fall in love with reading
» Get a mobile app that provides an ACT/SAT question every day
» Take practice tests often (such as a single section over a weekend)

My sons began their preparation for the SAT in the 8th grade by completing one untimed practice section a month. During the summer before 9th grade, they switched to one practice section a week. In October of their 9th and 10th grade years, they took the official SAT at the same location where they would eventually take the exam. I instructed them to relax and just answer each question to the best of their ability, with no blind guesses. Taking the test this early was done so that in the 11th and 12th grades, when it really mattered, they would be familiar and comfortable with the environment. They also began answering the SAT Question of the Day during their freshman years. Not surprisingly, they would miss a day every now and then, but they could answer additional questions to make up for it. The constant exposure helped them to master the various types of questions that they would encounter on the test. This approach is how my sons obtained SAT scores in the 1500s.

Start ACT/SAT prep early and work on it often. This repetition is important to gain familiarity of various types of test questions. Imagine a student's readiness if they take five minutes to answer and review one question a day over the span of three years! It does not matter how often you practice if it is not done properly; bad practice has little value over no practice. *Preparing for the ACT/SAT is less about getting the right answers and more about learning the correct strategies.* If your family plans to use an ACT or SAT prep course, be sure to choose one that prioritizes teaching techniques and strategies for answering the different styles of questions on the test.

Special Note: The costs associated with the ACT and SAT can be a burden for some families. It is, however, possible to obtain fee waivers for both taking the test and sending your scores to colleges. Reach out to your professional school counselor as your point of contact for requesting a waiver. Even if you are home-schooled, you can get fee waivers by contacting your local high school counselor (you must be enrolled in an accredited home school program).

It is important to review all answers on your practice tests. I have seen students make the mistake of not reviewing questions that they answered correctly. Do not skip this step just because you got the question right. Your correct response could have been the result of a guess or the use of a strategy that is unreliable for other questions.

I will have *a lot* more to say about both of these subjects as we progress through the book. **Be sure to read ALL sections regarding the ACT/SAT as each one will provide additional valuable insights.** Once you choose to take the official ACT or SAT, please see the College Email Account section at the end of this chapter before you register.

ACT/SAT Score Tracking

It is helpful to track you progress from year to year by recording your scores from either an official test, a practice test offered by a third party, or from a simulated test you conduct yourself. If testing independently, you can *estimate* your score by using the Raw Score Conversion Table on College Board's website or the Sample ACT Scoring Chart on The Princeton Review's website.

Freshman Essentials—Taking Flight

Grade Point Average (GPA)

The two most well-known metrics that colleges evaluate for admissions are the ACT/SAT score and GPA. Therefore, it is important to have a good understanding of how a GPA works in high school.

GPA is calculated by dividing the total amount of grade points earned by the total amount of credit hours attempted:

$$\frac{\text{Total Points Earned}}{\text{Total Credits Attempted}} = \text{GPA}$$

The most common scales range from 0.0 to 4.0 or 0 to 100. The standard 4.0 point-scoring system is:

Grade	Percentage	Points
A	90–100	4.0
B	80–89	3.5
C	70–79	2.0
D	60–69	1.0
F	00–59	0.0

Here is an example of a student's transcript with their earned grades, credit hours, and grade points:

Sample Transcript			
Course	Grade	Credit Hours	Grade Point
Biology	A	5	5 x 4 = 20
Algebra	B	5	5 x 3 = 15
Language Arts	A	5	5 x 4 = 20
U.S. History	A	5	5 x 4 = 20
French	B	5	5 x 3 = 15
Band	A	4	5 x 4 = 20
Credit Hours Attempted: 29			**110**

Referring back to the basic formula above, the student's total grade points earned (110) divided by their attempted credits (29) means the student has a GPA of 3.8.

$$\frac{110 \text{ Points Earned}}{29 \text{ Credits Attempted}} = 3.8 \text{ GPA}$$

This is how your grade point average will be calculated every semester, and your cumulative GPA is calculated in the same manner using all the courses on your transcript. The ranking of grade point averages amongst your class members is how the valedictorian and salutatorian is determined as well as your ranking in your graduating class.

The Ownership Shift

Up until this point, many of the things you accomplished have been the result of the parental "because I said so" philosophy. Most of what younger children achieve comes from the pushing and urging of a parent who knows what is best for them. During this next stage called high school, it is important for you to start taking ownership of your pursuits and find value in the opportunity for an education.

As you begin your ascent into adulthood, the simple desire to please your parent becomes less rewarding. The adults in your life can repeatedly tell you how important your education is, but until you understand the value of an education, you will rarely put forth your best effort. Even adults do not give their best effort without some benefit resulting from their work. An academically attractive college-bound student must want to pursue knowledge for their own benefit. **This shift in ownership begins with a plan.**

This book is intended as a model to help you navigate high school in order to become a highly sought-after college applicant. Having a plan for the future is essential, but it is even more important for the plan to be owned by you, not your parent. Your parent should serve as a guide by asking you thought-provoking questions and offering wisdom for consideration.

From my experience, here is a potential approach for building your plan:

1. **A vision statement**—Your vision statement should focus on tomorrow and captures your hopes and dreams. I like creating visions that define major milestones in life. Graduating high school and college are big milestones, but they are designed for the purpose of building towards your *"next"*. For the purpose of this book, I suggest something along the lines of envisioning your ideal job, your ideal living place, and maybe your ideal family situation.
2. **A mission statement**—Your mission statement should focus on today and captures your purpose and motivation. It should incorporate your dedication to build and execute a plan that is aligned with *your* vision. Your motivation to accomplish the vision should also be included. It should be expected that

the motivation will be unique to each student, derived from exclusive attributes. **Only *you* can determine how you will be inspired, not your parent**.

3. **Vision milestones**—The journey to your vision should be divided into milestones that mark a major chapter in your life that is required to be completed in order to achieve your final vision. Instead of just stating the milestone, allow it to include the route you will take, along with the requirements needed to achieve the vision milestone.
4. **Long-term goals**—Most milestones will take more than a few months to accomplish, so it is wise to define the steps necessary to reach your milestones as long-term goals.
5. **Short-term goals**—Interim goals should be set that build towards completing a long-term goal (or a milestone). The time frame for short-term goals is ideally around 30, 60, or 90 days. All goals should have a clear end date and have measures for success. This is important for building and executing an effective plan.
6. **Action plans**—State exactly what action needs to be taken to accomplish each short-term goal.
7. **A scorecard**—Measure your progress for each task in the action plan by defining relevant metrics. During each review of the plan, update the percentage of completion for each goal.

Given this approach to planning, allow me to suggest some ideas on how to begin your plan. Your vision is the catalyst for your plan but developing it can be tough for a ninth grader. It is not possible to dream about something that you do not even know exists. Research a variety of career fields and then pick a few that may be of interest. Allow your parent to provide suggestions based on their observations of your various interests. Then for your vision milestones, begin to look into the path it will take to obtain these careers. You may not be able to home in on a specific career at this point, and even if you do, it is perfectly normal for it to change a few times over the years. The reason for doing this as early as 9th grade is to begin envisioning your future. Envisioning your future is needed in order to build a plan to get there.

In the Freshman Focus section, I asked you a series of questions about your ideal future. The first version of your plan can be as general as the responses you gave in that section, or a bit more specific based on the research mentioned in the prior paragraph. Here is an example of how to build your plan:

- » The vision can be based off your dream job, dream house, and dream family.
  - › My vision is to have an upper-middle class income as a senior executive that will allow me to live in a nice neighborhood in a large city with warm weather near a beach.
- » The vision milestones will logically be defined in reverse order. Here is a generic sample for one part of the vision:
  - › I will attain my dream job with the skills and aptitude to train to become an executive.
  - › The route to my dream job will be via the completion of a professional degree with high standings.
  - › Acceptance to my professional school will require an undergraduate degree with high grades, experience in my field, and community involvement.
  - › I will attend a college well-respected for my intended major, and I will begin college with a financial plan that will leave me with little to no debt.
  - › At the end of my high school career, I will present myself as a very strong candidate on my college and scholarship applications.
  - › At the end of my high school career, I will be a college-ready student prepared to successfully complete college with honors.

Ninth Grade—Buying In

- » Long-term goals are required because each milestone will take time. Using this book, along with your independent research, you will be able to set these goals. Here are just a few examples for the vision milestone about being a strong college candidate:
    - › Develop and demonstrate leadership with meaningful results
    - › Develop and demonstrate my passion
    - › Develop the discipline required to be successful at the college level
    - › Score well on the ACT/SAT/PSAT
- » Short-term goals can be found throughout the Timeline sections of this book. I do expect you to do additional research to find other ideas. These examples support the goal of demonstrating leadership which are taken from the Extracurricular section of the Freshman Timeline:
    - › September 15—Research clubs or organizations of interest
    - › October 15—Attend one meeting for each club or organization of interest
    - › October 31—Final decision for which one(s) to join

This is a live plan that should adjust as you progress through high school. As you learn more about yourself and your aspirations, your milestones will change, goals will be adjusted, and new ones should be added. As goals change, the action plan and metrics to measure them will too. Therefore, I highly encourage reviewing the plan on a monthly basis to keep it active and fresh, which creates opportunities for adjustments to be made. I know monthly reviews may seem like a lot, but I encourage you to strive for it. Putting the plan on a board or wall where the entire family can see it often helps as motivation, especially if the board includes the value and the end goals of the plan.

By becoming a strong college applicant (the four wheels) and college-ready (the car), you will be ready to drive off to your dream college. Your plan is what keeps you organized and moving towards your dreams (vision). Your plan is the engine to the car you are building. With no engine, the best you can do is hope that a tow truck will get you to your destination, which means:

» The cost to get to your preferred college destination may be too high
» You may not be able to get to your preferred college destination
» You may have to just settle on the most convenient college destination

Most students have generic reasons for caring about their education or only pursue their studies out of an obligation to a parent. Here are some typical answers I hear from students when I ask why they go to school every day:

"Because I have to"	"Because my parent makes me"
"To get an education"	"To get a job"
"To graduate"	"To learn"

At face value, some of these reasons may seem valid, but they all lack a purposeful plan to achieve a greater goal. When you create a plan for your future goals, your *"why"* will be revealed!

Your *"why"* is an understanding of the reasons for each and every step you take today as they help you progress toward your tomorrow with purpose. Once you have created a plan, your eyes will sparkle when someone asks you a question that allows you to reveal your *"why."* This plan will allow you to take ownership of your educational pursuits, which will serve as a motivating factor throughout high school. *Remember, motivation is the first "Element of Discipline" in the development of discipline which is required for a college-bound student.*

Your plan will provide a vision into your future. A vision then generates hope for this future because you will then believe that you can achieve your goals. Belief and hope are the mindsets that will motivate you to take self-ownership. Your parent will not have to wake you up for school or push you to do your best. You will buy in to your education because you will see the value in why you are going to school. You will want to do the steps in this book because you will see the importance of a good (and hopefully free!) college education. This is the transition of ownership, the beginning of education with a purpose. Your plan is the foundation for the wonderful life that you dream for yourself.

Mindset of Excellence

> *"Doing the best at this moment puts you in the best place for the next moment."*
> *–Oprah Winfrey*

When I was a kid, my father had two sayings that have served me well in life:

- » "If you are going to bother to do something, do it right and to the best of your ability."
- » "If any other person has successfully done something, then why can't you?"

These statements instilled in me both excellence and confidence. The effect of excellence is long-standing, which is why I created a culture of excellence in my household.

Let's talk about what is meant by a culture of excellence. A culture of excellence fosters a mindset where you give your very **best effort** to every task that you do. The key to adopting this mindset is understanding that there are many factors that determine your best effort. Here are a few definitions that need to be clarified before we proceed:

> - **Optimal effort** entails *putting the maximum level* of an individual's capability into a task under ideal conditions.
> - **Maximum achievement** describes the *result* of your actions when putting forth your optimal effort.
> - **Perfection** is a flawless output that can be independent of the effort put in or the ability of any individual.

I want to be clear that "best effort" is *not* perfection. *Giving your best effort refers to what you put into a task and is the only aspect we have control over,* whereas achieving perfection is the outcome that we do not have total control of. Perfection can be an objective measurement or a subjective set of defined criteria. It is impossible to always have control over the outcome of our efforts due to unforeseen circumstances. Therefore, the desire to be consistently flawless can be dangerous for mental health.

A mindset of excellence recognizes that your best effort is only equivalent to your optimal effort under ideal conditions. However, we regularly have to deal with less than perfect situations. **"Best effort" is a mindset that does not allow for things outside of your control to serve as an excuse for not trying**. What constitutes putting forth your "best effort" changes based upon the circumstances you face at any given moment. When practice lasted all day and there is a mound of homework, "best effort" is not making excuses but figuring out how to efficiently get the most possible work done and then working with teachers to make up assignments. "Best effort" recognizes that a good research paper will require time management versus a last-minute scramble.

> **Parents**: My children knew that excellence was the standard in our household and that there was an expectation to always give their best effort. However, it was important that I considered every task and assignment independently while allowing them to explain any conditions that affected their "best effort."

Listening to my boys and understanding their circumstances was vital. I wanted to ensure that I did not apply too much pressure, which may have otherwise stressed them out. In situations where they clearly gave their best effort, I would be mindful to congratulate them even when I knew they did not perform up to their optimal effort.

Another particularly important factor is that I understood the uniqueness of each child. I knew the "best effort" from my eldest, Christopher, might result in a 78% on a calculus test, but I would question the "best effort" from my youngest, Aaron, if a math test resulted in a 92%. Even though my eldest's strong suit was not in math, his mindset of excellence allowed him to put forth his best effort because he recognized that everything he did mattered. On the other hand, my middle son Brian was a natural learner and instinctively had a mindset of excellence early on in his high school career that I believe was encouraged by a great set of friends that held one another accountable.

Everything You Do Matters

At first glance, the statement "everything you do matters" seems daunting and can create high levels of anxiety in a student. Putting forth your best effort can help mitigate the feeling of anxiety. School should not be a competition, but because of the way it was designed, this is what it has unfortunately become. Students lose focus when they compete to have one of the highest GPAs rather than valuing the art of learning and becoming well-rounded individuals. My wife and I stressed to our kids that the rankings will sort themselves out if they focus on doing their best and representing the best of who they are. At the end of your high school journey, you should not have to look back with any regrets.

Before The Application

My youngest son Aaron is a bright kid, but I can think of several other students from his class that were just as bright and well-rounded. Still, he was the one that gave the valedictory speech at graduation. One of the reasons he and a couple of other students immediately separated themselves from the rest of the pack is that they started off strong in their freshman year. Other students gained momentum during their sophomore year, and by junior year some even performed slightly better overall than my son. But the advantage of a strong start and a continued mindset of excellence allowed him to stay at the top of his class until the end.

Ask a senior who is applying to college, and they will tell you how much they now care about the effects their early high school years had on their college profile. Most will talk about how much they wish they had tried harder in a course as a freshman or studied harder for an exam as a sophomore. They will confess that they allowed extenuating circumstances to serve as excuses for subpar work on too many occasions. When the difference between letter grades is as simple as missing a couple of homework assignments, performing poorly on just one test because you were too tired to study, or procrastinating on that one essay because social media took up too much time, any senior would look back with regrets.

The issue is that most freshmen start high school without a concern for the competition involved in college admissions because they do not understand the consequences of their immediate actions. All eighth and ninth grade students should have a conversation with a senior in high school who has applied to college or a current college freshman who recently went through the application process. I suggest asking if they think it is important to put forth their "best effort" at every step of high school and see what they say. These older students can share what they wish they had done differently to positively impact their GPA and college profile.

Special Note: Some of you may not know a senior or college freshman that you can speak to. I am sure you are not the only freshman in the same predicament. If your school or community does not have a mentorship program, create one where conversations like this can take place. Establish an environment where upperclassmen can share their experiences and the lessons they have learned.

Most colleges have application deadlines between mid-December and mid-January with early admissions deadlines starting in October. This means that many colleges are primarily evaluating the first three years of high school for college decisions and, more importantly, college scholarships. ACT/SAT scores and GPA are among the most decisive metrics that come into play when comparing students to each other. When you decide from the beginning to always put forth your best effort, it gives you an advantage over those who may have settled too often in high school. This is a result of the way the higher education admissions process works. Colleges have a finite number of students they can admit, but the amount of applications that meet the necessary criteria far exceed this limit. So, colleges are not only deciding whether each individual student is qualified for admission, but more importantly, they have to decide which of the eligible students they will offer acceptance letters.

The goal is to be able to look at yourself in the mirror and feel confident that you gave it your *best effort*. Then when you apply to college, you will not need to compare yourself to others because you will know that you are getting the best opportunities for yourself. Therefore, it is important to understand that everything you do that can be rated or graded will be used by colleges when you apply: GPA, ACT/SAT, AP/IB exam scores, leadership, interests, etc. The process of obtaining excellence in these areas starts on the first day of class in high school. Do not feel that everything you do must be perfect yet be purposeful in everything you do!

Parents: Please remember to recognize the difference between best effort and perfection! Also, understand that there may be times when your child may need a mental health break, so do not punish them for the occasional lapse. Instead, empathize with them during these times and then encourage them to go forward.

Mental Health

When adopting an attitude where everything you do matters, you can always feel good about the effort you put in. Pairing this with a mindset of excellence is a very strong recipe for success. These attributes lead to becoming a high performer in all aspects of life, but sometimes this comes at a price. High performers are more susceptible to becoming overwhelmed and overstressed which is why it is important for students and parents to do regular checkups on mental health.

I asked a graduating senior from the class of 2020, Julia Seay, to assist me with this topic. She started the Brainy Bunch at Westlake High School (Atlanta), a program dedicated to creating a safe high school environment allowing students to receive counsel for mental health issues. Julia and her friends can be found on social media @braintothebunch or by email (thebrainybunch20@gmail.com). I will refer to her advice in a few sections of this book under the heading of "Julia Says."

Julia Says

I am sure you are looking for one grand solution for managing your mental health while still being successful in school. The secret is that there is not one universal way to accomplish this. Some people will say you should meditate or listen to music, but everyone is different in what they need as a person and as a student. As you flip through these mental health sections, you will learn that the key to your mental health and success is self-discovery: uncovering and figuring out who you are and what you can accomplish. In short, making an effort to find out what makes you, you.

To be mentally healthy and successful in high school, you must find a regiment that works well for you. Are you a night owl or an early bird? When are you the most energetic? Most importantly, how essential is sleeping to you and when do you need it most? For me, when I got home after school, I would not get anything done because I was irritable and stressed. Over time I realized that I was the most productive at night after taking a nap because I was no longer tired. Additionally, you need to discover which methods work best for managing the workloads of your classes, so figure out what makes handling your work easier for you. I found that seeing everything in an array of colors made my work more fun and organized. Discover if you need music or if you simply need to make to-do lists. Again, taking charge of your mental wellness is about figuring out who you are and what you need as a student and a person. As far as time management goes, the same idea applies.

Time management is key to your success and your mental wellness because it dictates how much you can do in a day. How you decide to manage your time depends on how far you can safely push yourself. Pushing yourself too far will cost you your mental wellness, but not pushing yourself enough will cost you success in high school. You have to set time ranges for when you sleep, eat, work, study, and have fun. I know it is easier said than done, but the first step is knowing your limits and gradually pushing them over the next four years. Ask yourself, how late can I stay up for these assignments? How long do I need to study the material? How long does it take until I reach my limit? Discovering this will help you develop time management skills that are tailored to you.

Parents: Clearly, I pushed my children to dream big, set ambitious goals, and work hard to achieve them. Even though I had high expectations, I also understood the importance of mental health. I want to share some things I believe to be very important when raising high-achieving children.

> - Approach them periodically for the sole purpose of seeing how they are doing.
> - Be observant and look for any strange changes in behavior.
> - Help them avoid any undue stress by not allowing them to chase after perfection.
> - Take the time to understand your child so that you do not place more on them than they can handle.
> - Plan for regular conversations with a focus on listening to them and allowing them to voice their concerns.
> - Pour positive remarks into them more often than you give criticism. Your kids need to hear that you are proud of them.
> - Remember that excellence has room for mistakes.

Discipline—Focus on Time Management

Time management is the second "Element of Discipline" in the development of discipline. It is important to start here because it is the most difficult skill for a teenager to cultivate and one that even many adults struggle with.

> *"In order to maintain study skills, one of the most important factors in college is time management. Without it, many other important areas such as studying or leisure cannot stay in balance. Time is*

one of our most important resources. Effective time management is a skill most people need to make the most out of their personal and professional lives. To a college student, it can make the difference between a mediocre and a superior performance."

–Wright State University

Most high school and college students tend to wait until "crunch time" before completing the bulk of an assignment. While this is clearly not the best practice, many students fail to see the impact of procrastination on the quality of their work and therefore do not respect the value of time management. Now that you understand that everything you do matters, it is just as important to realize that *how* you go about doing things can significantly affect the results of *everything* you do. It is not always easy to identify the cause of bad results, but all too often, the lack of time management is the culprit for failing to put forth optimal effort.

Here is a practical exercise that can be used to help understand the cost of procrastination. Write a 750-word report or essay on any topic or book. (This is less than 2 pages.) Schedule a date to do your writing, and the day before, decide on a topic and a start time. Allow 2-4 hours to write the paper depending on how much time you think you will need. Once you finish writing, set aside your essay for a few days, but no longer than a week. This period of time will allow you to have a fresh perspective on your work. The next step is to review the paper with a parent or someone you trust to evaluate your writing and critique it for content, flow, errors, and clarity. For most students, it will be apparent that the paper is not reflective of their best effort due to the time constraint. This exercise demonstrates that proper time management provides ample time to review and make necessary adjustments to ensure quality work.

Special Note: By the way, this exercise is not time wasted on your part! In addition to learning the lesson of time management, you are practicing writing an essay which is an important part of the college application process. I would even suggest making the necessary corrections to the paper. Overall, it is a great exercise and can serve as an assessment of your essay writing skills.

I spoke earlier about the culture of excellence that was established in my household. But let me be clear... my kids did NOT like the hardships of learning time management in any shape or form, particularly my oldest son, who resisted the most. However, he has just completed law school, which requires more discipline than just about any other field of study. My other two sons are in the midst of their undergraduate education and definitely have a handle on time management, although they still have their moments of procrastination. The difference is that they now know when they can get away with it versus when it will cost them.

Parents: With my kids always striving to deliver their optimal effort, we periodically assessed major assignments and exams while they were in high school. I had them create a plan of action in preparation for upcoming tasks, followed by a review to determine if they adhered to the plan and if it yielded the desired results. This allowed me to ascertain whether they were struggling in a subject and needed assistance or if there was a time management issue that needed to be addressed. If the latter was true, and most of the time this was the case, there needed to be consequences to make them reflect on the impact of their lack of discipline. Unless it was a chronic issue, the consequences did not have to be anything major. I am a proponent of the idea that occasionally losing screen time at a young age is worth it if it teaches the kids the discipline of time management, a skill that has value for a lifetime.

Freshman Timeline— Starting with Purpose

START OF SCHOOL YEAR

Extracurricular Activities

There was a time when colleges wanted to see students involved in a long list of extracurricular activities to demonstrate their "well-roundedness." This is no longer the case. **Colleges now want to see impactful leadership, community service, and demonstrated passion (or strong interest).** This can be accomplished through participation in any of the following activities: clubs, sports, scouts, third-party programs, etc. Leadership, service, and passion will be integral parts of your college applications, college essays, and scholarship essays. Recognizing this now is invaluable because the sooner you understand the college admissions process, the more time you will have to build an attractive application. Let me illustrate some important aspects of leadership, community service, and demonstrated passion:

> **Impactful Leadership**—I often see high school resumés where the student simply lists their leadership roles. When targeting certain colleges, and especially when targeting scholarships, leadership titles are considered a minimum standard. The value, however, comes from being able to demonstrate what the student accomplished in that role and how they were able to make a difference. Leadership opportunities can come from many different avenues such as leading a club, starting up or working with a non-profit organization, scouts service projects, etc. **The key is being able to show how your leadership resulted in a meaningful impact.**

Aaron was president of the Math Club. He and a friend re-established the club after a 2-year absence from the high school. He revitalized the club by visiting math competitions to gain experience, trained fellow math club members to compete, and then worked with his school to host a math competition. He even organized the fundraising to substantially finance the event. This display of leadership provides more value than simply stating, "I was president of the Math Club."

Community Service—Colleges will ask about your involvement in detail. I have my theories as to why colleges care so much about community service:

1. The college experience revolves around community. Engaging in community service throughout high school shows colleges that you care about your community and want to contribute towards its success. Colleges seek out this type of student because they will help build a vibrant atmosphere on campus.
2. Colleges want to see what is meaningful to you, which may help determine if you are a good fit for their culture.
3. Most importantly, what type of alumni does a college want? Ones that want to give back to the school after they graduate. Colleges recognize that a student who values community service is more likely to give back.

Start now by getting involved in things that are meaningful to you and in doing so, you may eventually discover an opportunity to make a difference. Taking this initiative can even turn your volunteer work into a potential leadership opportunity. Being able to write passionately about your leadership in meaningful community activities will be advantageous when applying for scholarships.

Like most college-bound students should, Aaron was able to list many hours of community service on his application. As an added bonus, he was able to find opportunities whose value extended beyond the benefits of volunteering. For example, he volunteered with local professionals to build websites for non-profits in his community, which was another way for him to show experience in his chosen major of computer science. Also, he volunteered as a musician at a local church, which helped demonstrate commitment to his personal passion.

Demonstrated Passion—In years past, a "well-rounded" student seemed to be defined mostly by the number of activities they were involved in. I participated in over 20 different extracurricular activities throughout my four years of high school. An Ivy League school's admissions counselor told me how impressed they were with this number and how it helped to overcome my GPA and SAT score being lower than their typical applicants'. Today, colleges are more interested in quality over quantity. They want to see a student demonstrate how they were able to "make their mark" on something they are passionate about (or at least show a strong interest in). I have seen this done successfully through several avenues:

Academic programs—Consider one or two areas of personal interests, and I am confident that you will find a variety of after-school, weekend, or summer programs for you to be involved in throughout high school. The experiences you will gain through such academic programs could even lead to discovering your passions. Regardless, the key is to show colleges that you are committed to your interests by actively engaging with them.

Nonprofits/Organizations—Being able to say that you started a nonprofit or business organization looks great on your college application. For it to serve as your demonstrated passion, you need to be able to show how it has made a difference. I personally know a student who successfully started an organization that began at his local high school, branched out to the entire school system, and was ultimately adopted by the state superintendent. He then started a nonprofit to help other students create their own businesses. I am also acquainted with a student who started two organizations, one of which gained an international presence. They made a difference with their organizations, which largely contributed to why they are both currently students at Stanford University. You can generate ideas for your potential organization by looking for a need in your school, community, or city and then finding a way to address it.

Sports—While being committed to a sport for years can be a positive thing, understand that colleges will also want to know how you were able to excel at that sport. They want to see leadership roles (i.e. team captain), national rankings, recruitment letters, or major accomplishments. Sports participation is a supporting element of an educational experience. Colleges prefer not having to be concerned about whether their student athletes will remain academically eligible. Therefore, performing well in the classroom and on standardized tests can help you get a scholarship offer over a slightly better athlete. Unless you are a Blue Chip athlete, a low GPA and ACT/SAT score will cause you to miss out on the better college offers.

Of course, there are other ways to demonstrate passion or a strong interest. No matter how you choose to do it, you need to "make your mark" with something that is meaningful to you in order to set yourself apart. There is no age limit for creating change or having a meaningful impact in your community. When teens create a mindset for making the world a better place, you are only ensuring a brighter future for you to live in.

Ninth Grade—Buying In

Aaron was fortunate enough to be able to demonstrate his passion through multiple mechanisms. As I discuss in other sections, he involved himself in many programs that demonstrated his love for mathematics. He also created a non-profit organization to fill a need at his school along with his brother Brian. Finally, he is an avid drummer who attended multiple summer music camps and regularly played with his high school jazz band, with a jazz group that performed professionally at local venues, and at his church as a volunteer.

Freshmen should use extracurricular activities to start exploring potential interests within and outside of your school. You will want to join a couple of clubs or organizations now, even if you do not have a lot of time to commit, because starting early provides a better opportunity for leadership roles in the years to follow. Be careful not to get overinvolved, because for the first few months of high school, you will be getting acclimated to your new environment.

Special Note: Your transcript informs a prospective college of your fulfillment of the prerequisite courses required. The Grade Point Average (GPA) provides an understanding of your level of mastery of the content from the classes on your transcript. The score that you earn on the ACT/SAT will be a measure of how well you can apply information you have learned. However, while your GPA and college entrance exam score are enough to prove that you qualify for acceptance to a particular college, these metrics alone are not the best gauges of your ability to handle the rigors of college and overcome obstacles that may come your way. Once a school has determined your aptitude, the best indicator for success is *grit*; consequently, how can a college measure grit? A significant factor colleges use to assess grit is to consider your demonstrated passion. This factor can show that you are willing to go beyond the norms and demonstrate how far you are willing to go to overcome obstacles in order to accomplish your goals. **Even if you are not targeting an upper echelon college or university, making a commitment in this area is what puts you in an advantageous position to be awarded** *scholarship money!*

Before The Application

Logging Activities, Programs, Awards, and Honors

Creating an Activity Log is something you will be glad you did when it is time to fill out college and scholarship applications. I suggest creating a document to record anything and everything you participate in or accomplish throughout your high school career. (It could also be useful when creating a high school resumé!) While it is ideal to log items as they occur, set a reminder to alert you at least twice a year to record items while they are fresh on your mind. When my sons were in school, we created an Excel spreadsheet* with a tab for each child. It included the following information:

Date/Range: The month and year of the activity, program, award, or honor (Include the start and end dates of programs and activities where appropriate)

Name: Name of the activity, program, award, or honor

Description: Detailed explanation of the activity, program, award, or honor

Value: Brief description of what you learned, what you contributed, how you were impacted, and the difference you made regarding the activity or program

Leadership: Any title or leadership role held

Hours: Number of hours per week spent on the program or activity (on average)

A template for this spreadsheet can be downloaded for free at woolfolkworks.com/templates

The following example is an excerpt from Aaron's activity log:

Date	07/15/18	11/01/18	01/04/19	06/24/19	
End Date	11/15/18	04/23/21	02/29/19	07/05/19	
Name	Marching Band	School Jazz Band	Upward Basketball Volunteer	GSU Rialto Jazz Camp	Georgia Tech
Frequency	Daily	Daily	Weekly	Daily	Daily
Hours	10/week	2–4/week	4/week	80	80
Description	Snare drummer	Drumset	Game clock operator; assistant coaching	Jazz training by professionals	Worked alongside a Georgia Tech math professor looking to answer the question, "What time does the sun set and rise?"
Value		Develop passion; awarded role as a freshman	Positive role model for your boys in the community; promote safe environment	Develope passion	I was able to challenge myself by using math to solve a real-world problem and make friends in the process
Leadership	N/A	Primary Drummer	N/A	N/A	N/A

Throughout the college application process, you will be asked to write about your activities, programs, awards, and honors many times and in various forms. You will likely refer to this document when writing essays for college and scholarship applications. Most applications will also require you to list each item along with a summary describing them. They will ask you for the number of hours spent per week and the range of weeks (number of weeks per year) of your activity to determine how much time you have invested into each activity. Keep this in mind when you decide to participate in various activities as you will want to have at least one undertaking that demonstrates significant involvement.

This section of your application will afford you an opportunity to use your experiences to express your passions and strong interests, and doing this will be much easier if you have taken the time to log the value of all of your activities since ninth grade. Do not underestimate this portion of the application. The ability to portray your story may just be what puts you ahead of comparable students also applying to your target schools or even give you a chance at your stretch schools. So, create this document now and keep it up to date. You will appreciate having everything documented when time comes.

THANKSGIVING BREAK

Evaluation Time

The transition to high school is quite different for every student, and a strong start in freshman year goes a long way towards the fulfillment of the concept of "everything you do matters." Not all students get the start they want at the beginning of high school. Unfortunately, many of them struggle in silence, hoping that the situation will magically resolve itself or may not even realize that they are struggling. Students that attempt to make adjustments without seeking help may find the road to recovery to be long and difficult.

For these reasons, I suggest an evaluation period sometime before the Thanksgiving holiday (during fall break for those that have one). Use this time to evaluate the first few months of high school. It is important for you to share with a parent what you believe is going well and what is not. Express how you feel about your classes, teachers, and classmates. If you do not feel comfortable having these conversations face-to-face, I encourage you to share your thoughts by writing them down. You should partner together to make the necessary adjustments for a better plan of action moving forward.

> **Parents**: It is very important to spend less time talking and more time listening; you should not only listen but truly hear what your student is saying; you should not only hear their words but receive them from the perspective of a ninth grader

who does not have your life experience and wisdom. Then you must trust that your child will hear your guidance and also allow them to adapt your recommendations in a way that works for them. If you do not feel that you have the experience and wisdom to help them make adjustments, I suggest partnering with their counselor for assistance.

This exercise of trust not only serves to help you rebound from a less than ideal start, but it also helps your parent ease up and allow you to grow and mature. Working together, you learn to take ownership of your education while respecting your parent's input and assistance.

During this time of evaluation, you should also work together to assess any activities or programs you have joined or plan to join during freshman year:

- » Ensure that participation in extracurricular activities is properly prioritized to not conflict with classwork.
- » When looking for activities to join that fit best, have a conversation with your parent regarding your interest in different types of activities, clubs, and programs.
- » Then evaluate your potential interests while giving serious consideration to suggestions from your parent.

It is important that you find what it is you are interested in beyond high school and begin to develop that skill before you apply to college.

CHRISTMAS BREAK

Research Summer Programs

In order to become a strong college applicant, you want to take full advantage of all three summers of high school. There is a wide range of in-person summer programs that can last anywhere from one week to a couple of months and may be offered as commuter or overnight programs. Most of these programs provide a great opportunity to deeply explore a field of interest. Program topics range from leadership, academic research, arts, STEM (robotics, coding, game design), social, music, etc. The typical high school senior will choose their college major with little to no personal experience but exploring your fields of interest can help provide a basis for your decision. (There are also great programs that teach leadership skills that may be of interest to you.)

Many of these in-person summer programs come with a hefty price tag, but there are plenty that have little to no cost at all. Not surprisingly, these programs fill up quickly. Hence, you should start your research early so that you will have a head start for snagging the best and most cost-effective program for the upcoming summer. You will also have time to request items from your school that programs may require, such as transcripts and letters of recommendation. Begin your research before Christmas break by talking to teachers at your school that may have connections to special programs.

Use your time during the break to explore opportunities. Here are a few tips:

- » A general search for "summer programs for high school students" or "summer programs for teens" should provide results in your area.
- » Colleges across the country offer summer programs for high school students, so explore the websites of your local or regional colleges.
- » Several websites such as *teenlife.com* and *fastweb.com* offer a list of local and national programs.

As you conduct your research, document website links, program dates, application start and end dates, and any requirements to complete the application. For free and low-cost programs, you want to apply within a few days of the application opening.

Ninth Grade—Buying In

My youngest son, Aaron loves math and had an interest in computer science. He attended a week-long math program at Georgia Tech during the summers after his freshman and junior years. He used these two experiences to respond to several prompts on college and scholarship applications. It did not matter that they were only a week long because he was able to document all the things he learned, his contribution to the projects, the value he gained from the experiences, and his ability to work well with others. He was also fortunate to be selected to attend a 4-week residential honors program where he specialized in math. His time there sparked a strong interest in proving his own original math theory. After an interview for a major college scholarship, one of the panelists was beaming while telling me how passionate my son was about math. His participation in these summer programs provided an opportunity for him to demonstrate his passion, which set him apart from other similarly qualified students. This distinction helped him to secure the scholarship.

In-person summer programs provide an added benefit of learning in a different environment outside of a high school building. This type of experience is beneficial so that starting college in four years is not your first exposure to learning in a new environment. You will also find plenty of online and virtual summer programs or classes offered for high school students. You may want to find a program or class that will strengthen your knowledge or allow you to get ahead in a school subject area for the upcoming school year. These types of courses are also great for learning a new skill or hobby.

Special Note: Any activity that you participate in is an opportunity to add to the Activities, Programs, Awards & Honors spreadsheet. This will be very valuable when filling out applications.

Before The Application

Future Senior Resumé

Never tell a child that the sky is the limit because you just may be talking to a future astronaut.

There are two types of resumés a high school student can have: professional and educational. The professional resumé is designed to be given to a potential employer in hopes of securing a job. The educational resumé is for college admissions and scholarship committees and is designed to summarize highlights from your high school career. As a freshman, create an educational resumé that you want to have as a senior three years from now. This exercise is useful in many ways. Doing research to complete your future resumé should help you discover fresh ideas for new goals. Setting goals that you can strive to achieve is a great way to hold yourself accountable. As stated before, taking advantage of this time of discovery is important because you cannot dream about something that you do not know even exists.

Your research should include reaching out to current or recent high school seniors that you respect to review their resumes for accomplishments that you may want to emulate. You will hopefully notice how much they vary as there is no one picture of success. As you build your own resumé, include your ideal GPA and desired ACT/SAT score. Do not include your desired class rank as it is not a standardized measure of success and is subject to factors outside of your control. List some awards and honors you wish to achieve and accomplishments from activities and programs you can see yourself participating in. This resumé is the vision for the plan you will be building and adapting throughout your high school career. Dare to think big and dream big! Keep this resumé in full view in your home as a motivational reminder. It should be fun to look back and compare it to your actual resumé during your senior year.

SPRING BREAK

College Majors

Not too long ago, deciding on a college major took place after your sophomore year in college. Today, many colleges expect students to choose an intended major when filling out their application. Thus, when you apply to a college, you are competing against the applicants who wish to pursue a similar program of study as yourself, not against every student who applies to the school.

This means that the applicants for the more sought-after majors (which vary by university) will face the toughest competition. Colleges break down their target enrollment numbers by discipline to maintain a proper balance of students. This ensures that there are enough available classes for each major. Since selecting your intended major is now a part of the college application and acceptance process, it is to your advantage to not wait until your senior year to begin considering your options.

Once enrolled in college, changing majors can often come at a cost, and there are no guarantees that you will be able to make a switch to your desired major. According to the National Center for Education Statistics (NCES), **"About one-third of students enrolled in bachelor's degree programs changed majors" and "about 1 in 10 students changed majors more than once."** Many universities will have a different set of core class requirements for each of their colleges, and classes previously completed may not apply towards a new major, which could ultimately delay graduation. **More time spent in college means more money paid towards tuition and other expenses.**

I have noticed that students often arbitrarily choose their majors. For many, the choice tends to come from subjects they liked in high school, what an authority figure—or the media they consumed—suggested they should do. College majors are typically chosen without considering the career it could lead to, but this method is flawed because it wrongly places the "cart before the horse." The purpose of college is to gain a marketable skill to take into the workforce, so this is where choosing a college major should start. To avoid selecting between a set of arbitrary options, now is the time to start exploring a variety of career fields that may be of interest to you. Doing so may not eliminate the possibility of changing majors, but it will reduce the odds.

While your favorite school subjects in high school should not be the sole basis for choosing your college major, they should be the starting point for your research into potential career fields. Over time, your interests will be influenced by people you speak with, new classes you take, programs you participate in, organizations you volunteer with, and other sources.

As you identify areas of interest, find a way to speak with or interview professionals in these areas. Learn about the different specialties that exist within their career field and the various facets of their specialty. Find out what they do on a day-to-day basis and see if you can imagine yourself doing the same. If you need ideas of questions to ask, the following list is a great place to start (these come from a non-profit organization that my sons Brian and Aaron created in high school to address this very need):

- » What are your post-secondary school and degree(s):
- » What company do you work for?
- » What are your work responsibilities?
- » What are the day-to-day tasks you have to do in order to fulfill these responsibilities?
- » What type of location do you work in?
- » What is the atmosphere of your job?
- » What do you like the most about your job?
- » What is the most rewarding part of your job?
- » What do you like the least about your job?
- » What was the career path that led to your current job? What are your future career goals?

- » What are some of the benefits or perks that come with your job?
- » What is the salary range for your job?
- » What school subjects and/or interests are related to this profession?
- » What advice would you give to a student interested in your profession?
- » What would you tell your high school self to do differently?
- » Is there anything else you would like to say about your profession?

If they are willing, spend some time shadowing them at work to get a firsthand glimpse into their world. This process should extend throughout your high school career, so becoming adept at this type of research now will make it easier to do later when you are much busier. By the start of your senior year, hopefully you will have done enough research to identify potential career fields that will translate into possible college majors. This is how you put the *horse before the cart*!

Summer Programs and Activities

By spring break, you should have already applied to a few summer programs. If so, be sure to follow up and confirm that everything is in order, and if not, it is time to investigate what may still be available. Students, please do not spend the entire summer with no plans. You should take time to rest and recuperate, but not for the whole summer. Also consider applying to camps or programs that promote healthy physical activities since a lot of teens lack the proper amount of physical activity in their daily lives. If your summer program or activity lasts less than a couple of weeks or you are not able to secure one, take this time to secure a part-time job while positions are still available. This alternative is valuable because work history is also well-received on college applications.

SUMMER BREAK

Summer Programs or Activities—Additional Ideas

Ideally, at least part of this summer is already planned, and you have a summer program(s) and/or job lined up. If not, consider including some of the alternative activities below:

- » READ!!! Find a couple of fun books to read over the summer. Many colleges ask, "What is one of your favorite books and why?" Consider resources such as the Helen Ruffin Reading Bowl Booklist and Project Lit.
- » Research online or virtual classes that may still be available.
- » Use online resources to learn a new skill.
- » Do volunteer work.
- » Develop a plan to address a problem in your school or community.
- » Create your own work opportunity (such as mowing lawns or babysitting).
- » Plan to create a new club at your school. This type of endeavor can be fun, especially when done with a friend or two.
- » Commit to a physical workout plan.

Keep in mind that these activities can also be used to supplement your existing plans. Make sure your schedule has plenty of time for rest and fun!

Essay Writing

Your personal statement essay will be an important part of your college application. Later in this book, I will provide you with tips and strategies on how to make yours stand out. Writing about yourself is not as easy as it seems. During this summer, I want you to get accustomed to writing an essay about yourself in the correct format using an actual college prompt. Here are your instructions:

- » Choose one of the following prompts that I adapted from The Princeton Review:
    1. **Describe a person you admire.**
       Write about how this person influenced you. Avoid the urge to pen an ode to a beloved figure like Gandhi or Abraham Lincoln. Instead, write about someone who has actually caused you to change your behavior or your worldview.
    2. **Discuss how you have learned from a challenge, setback, or failure.**
    3. Overcoming challenges demonstrates courage, grit, and perseverance! The obstacle you write about can be large or small, just be sure to show how your perspective changed as a result.
    4. **Share a story about your background, identity, interest, or talent that is very meaningful to you.**
    5. Answer this prompt by reflecting on a hobby, a facet of your personality, or an experience that is genuinely meaningful and unique to you. Use any topic as long as you can tie it back to who you are or what you believe in.
    6. **What topic, idea, or concept captivates you?**
    7. Explain how you pursue that interest by considering what or who you turn to when you want to learn more.
- » The essay should be between 500-700 words.
- » Assume you are writing the essay to a person who has no prior knowledge of you. The purpose of the personal statement essay is for the admissions officer to get a glimpse into who you are from your writing, so you must get personal.
- » Be sure that your essay is well-written, error-free, and has excellent grammar.

- » Do *not* follow the rigid five-paragraph essay format of an introduction, three main body paragraphs, followed by a conclusion. Your essay should flow as if you were telling a story to the reader.
- » Read it aloud to get a fresh perspective on how it sounds.
- » When you are done, have others read it and provide feedback. When you return to school, it may be possible to get more input from a language arts teacher or a school counselor.

ACT/SAT Focus

Let me reemphasize that even though some college admissions representatives and counselors downplay its significance, your ACT or SAT score matters. Let me put these scores into proper perspective:

- » Not every student can score in the 99th percentile, so please do not think I am suggesting that you must have a near perfect standardized test score.
- » Your ACT/SAT score must make you competitive for the schools you will eventually target, so you need to work towards obtaining your personal best score.
- » It is possible that your personal best scores may bring schools within reach that you may not have otherwise considered.
- » Your ACT/SAT score alone will *not* get you into most colleges (there are a few colleges that will accept you primarily based on your ACT/SAT score and GPA). However, falling short of your best possible ACT/SAT score ***can*** keep you from being accepted to your dream or stretch college.

Typically, most college-bound students have been exposed to over 90% of the content on these tests by the end of sophomore year. If this is true, you may wonder why most scores are not in the upper range. This is because these tests are not just about content, but also about

Ninth Grade—Buying In

the application of the content. If the questions were as simple as asking students to do algebra problems, there would be many high scores. Instead, the test is designed to determine if students can identify which concepts to apply and use them correctly. In other words, you are not just being tested on what the content is, but also if you understand the underlying principles (the "whys") behind the content.

Therefore, your approach to preparing for these tests can be your advantage because your prep will consist of more than simply taking a few practice tests a couple of weeks before the exam date. Your preparation will accomplish three goals:

- » Build up your acumen for determining how and when to apply the content to varying styles of questions.
- » Ensure you have a firm grasp on the content.
- » Familiarize yourself with the styles of questions on the test.

The steps you take to accomplish these goals should incorporate the following objectives:

- » Exposure—format of test, time constraints, testing environment, all styles of questions
- » Repetition—the more times you complete a specific type of question, the more comfortable you will be when answering it in the future. You have to work on ACT/SAT continuously and habitually.
- » Testing Strategies—provides the ability to efficiently identify correct answers which helps with overcoming time constraints, relieves stress, and builds confidence, leading to overall improved scores.
- » Practice—measure your progress by conducting regular timed test sections and enrolling in official tests prior to junior year. Alternatives: your school may offer official practice test days or you can simulate a test day on your own.

While there is no single method for accomplishing these goals and objectives, I will share what we did in our household that generated positive results.

I bought a reputable SAT practice book (because the SAT is the dominant test where we live) that provided detailed explanations in the answer section. Over the summer after freshman year, my boys explored one test section each week. The idea was not to find the answers to the problems, but to examine them. You may want to consider this approach each time you review a test section as a part of your prep strategy this summer:

Math:
1. Attempt to identify the math concept required to answer every question in a section,
2. e.g. equation of a line, factorization.
3. Indicate whether you know the skill(s) necessary to get the answer,
4. e.g. algebraic simplification, factoring, and algebra.
5. Take a few days to determine what strategies you would use to find the answers and then compare them to the strategies provided in the answer section.
6. Keep a running a list of all concepts, skills, and strategies you need to brush up on.

Writing and Language*:
1. Read the passage and any supplementary material.
2. Without looking at the questions, mark any grammatical errors or inconsistencies that you can identify.
3. Attempt to correct any grammatical errors you find to the best of your ability.
4. Questions in this section will reference a portion of the passage. For every question, compare the notes you made in steps 2 & 3 to the correct answer provided in the answer section.

Reading*:
1. Read the passage and any supplementary material.
2. Identify key literary elements such as tone, setting, theme, motifs, narrative point of view, etc. Indicate which lines in the passage support each element you identify.
3. Annotate the passage for figurative language such as metaphor, hyperbole, simile, personification, etc. Write down the idea that the figurative device conveys.
4. Some questions will ask about literary elements or figurative elements. For these questions, compare the notes you made in steps 2 & 3 to the correct answer provided in the answer section.
5. The remaining types of questions can only be prepared for by consistent exposure to a variety of reading material.

General reading comprehension is essential for both the Writing/Language and Reading sections. Therefore, the best preparation for these sections will always be regular reading.

Practicing strategies for answering questions on all sections is suggested during the summer after sophomore year. Your focus this summer will be on recognizing concepts through exposure and preparing to learn test question strategies. This work will be in addition to the repetition and practice gained from using some type of ACT or SAT app on your phone to answer at least one question a day. If you are not currently utilizing such an app, download one and start now.

For those who need even more motivation to spend the time to properly prepare for these tests, visit some college websites that provide information regarding their scholarship programs. This will help you get a better idea of why spending time to properly prepare for these tests is so important. You will notice that most schools highlight the GPAs and ACT/SAT scores of their major scholarship recipients. Besides having a mindset of excellence and an understanding that every assignment matters starting on the first day of high school, to get your ideal ACT/

SAT score, you must commit to putting in the necessary time. The old saying holds true: "If you want what other people do not have, you must be willing to do what most are not willing to do."

PSAT—In the fall, the College Board offers an annual Preliminary SAT (PSAT) designed for students of any grade to take before their senior year of high school. This test is offered for free by many schools and is a great litmus test for the actual SAT used for college entrance. You want to be sure to take advantage of these opportunities if you are fortunate enough to take the test for free.

During your junior year of high school, this same test is also used as the National Merit Scholarship Qualifying Test (NMSQT). As stated by The Princeton Review, "Some of the highest scoring students may win scholarship money, so while you shouldn't stress out about the PSAT, you certainly shouldn't ignore it either." Your score will need to be at least in the 97th percentile in the country to be in consideration for semi-finalist status, and then approximately the top 1% of each state are chosen to be finalists. My oldest son, Christopher, was awarded three full-ride scholarships simply based on his PSAT score. This should help you appreciate the advantage of starting your test prep at this early stage.

Discipline—Focus on Organization

In her article "Why Is it Important to Be Organized in College," Patrice Lesco pointed out that "college life is a fast-paced world in which you are required to become involved in your education and keep up with its demands. Yet, this can become difficult when papers, books, schedules and your life become cluttered. Organization, therefore, is a key factor to your survival and success in college."

Being organized is the third "Element of Discipline" to be covered in the development of discipline. In many cases, organization works hand in hand with time management. Oddly enough, there are people who struggle with organization and yet are good with time management and vice versa, so just because you are good with one does not mean you will not battle with the other. No matter your current level of organizational ability, make an effort this summer to improve in this area.

Your sophomore year of high school is a critical juncture, and the demands on your time will only continue to increase. Failure to handle the increased demands can potentially have negative implications. Together with your parent, conduct the appropriate research on how to build organizational skills that specifically suit you. You should develop and practice these skills this summer before entering your sophomore year.

Many schools provide planners to high school students or suggest that students purchase them because there are significant benefits to using them. I suggest utilizing one for the remainder of your high school journey. Using a planner can help you, and it gives parents another good tool to track your progress in school. You can ask for help from your parent if you are not sure how to use this great tool to be a more successful student. In her article "How Planners Help Students Learn Organizational Skills," Ann Logsdon states that planning is essential for several reasons:

- » It reduces stress
- » It reduces ineffective study habits such as cramming
- » It helps prevent learning disabled students from feeling overwhelmed
- » It increases productivity
- » It teaches a life skill that will be beneficial in the future.

(You can find the full article at *https://www.verywellfamily.com/teach-planning-and-organizational-skills-2162269*.)

I admit that my sons struggled in different ways with organizational skills throughout high school, but they learned how to cope. Christopher overcame this weakness with a very strong work ethic, while Brian was more of a natural at being organized. I was determined to make sure that a lack of organization was not a stumbling block once they entered college. I found a solution that is serving each one of them very well in college, which I will discuss in the Pre-College chapter. Unless you have other strengths that allow you to overcome a lack of organizational skills, make the development of these skills a priority now.

College Research

At this stage, you should already be doing preliminary college research. In all of the talks I have given, I have been alarmed by how many families with senior students do not understand the college application process or what it takes to be considered for admittance. The core application requirements for many colleges are fairly similar, but the remaining requirements can vary greatly for each college you apply to. At this time, I want you to simply educate yourself on the various style of colleges that you may want to target so that you will understand what you are working towards.

College portals—Previous generations had to fill out a separate application for every college they applied to. Today, many colleges utilize an application portal that gathers the most common data from an applicant, preventing the need to input the same data at multiple sites. Then each college will typically add any unique requirements once their school is selected. During this summer, you and your parent should familiarize yourselves with the application portals and review required application entries.

The most used portals as of this writing are the Common App and Coalition for College. While many schools are on both portals, the Common App seems to lean more heavily towards private schools while

Coalition trends more towards public schools. There is also a portal used by many of the Historically Black Colleges and Universities (HBCUs) called the Common Black College Application. Look at the various sections of the core application to gain an understanding as to what information they will be requesting, such as GPA, ACT/SAT score, extracurricular activities, leadership roles, summer activities, etc. Then, take note of the different prompts for the main essay section. Finally, select a few colleges you are familiar with to review the additional requirements they may request.

College requirements—While choosing potential colleges is still far off, it will be here before you know it. For research purposes, pick a few local colleges you may want to consider, as well as a few colleges farther away that you may be interested in. Visit each of their websites, take their virtual tours, and let the thought of going away to college in a few years get you excited about your future! Also take note of their average ACT/SAT scores and GPAs. These metrics are typically displayed in a range of the middle 50% from the last class of admitted students (25%-75%).

College financial aid—While visiting each of the college websites, be sure to explore both the financial aid and scholarship sections. According to *EducationalData.org*, the average yearly price of tuition, fees, room, and board for 2019-20 was $30,500 but can vary widely:

- » $21,950 for public 4-year institution (in-state rate)
- » $38,330 for public 4-year institution (out-of-state)
- » $49,879 for private nonprofit 4-year institution

The average total price for a 4-year degree is approximately $122,000.

- » $87,800 for a public 4-year institution (in-state rate)
- » $153,320 for a public 4-year institution (out-of-state)
- » $199,500 for a private nonprofit 4-year institution

These numbers point to the humongous debt many college graduates face. Many Americans are saddled with college debt that takes 30 years of their life to pay off. It is hard to buy a house when you are already making payments on college loans equal to a mortgage. If the website you are visiting has a cost calculator, work with your parent to use this tool to estimate what your out-of-pocket costs would be. Beyond helping you to become a strong college applicant, I also want to help you avoid having any significant debt when you graduate from college. As you visit the scholarship section of the school website, note the application requirements and the profile of the scholarship recipients. Doing so can serve as motivation for you to set your goals, create your plan, and take the necessary steps to achieve those goals.

Available resources—While I do encourage you to visit a variety of official college websites to get a feel for how to navigate them and gather information as a prospective student, there are other resources available for gathering statistics and data about schools. There are websites that provide school reports and school rankings by many different categories. A few examples are *usnews.com/best-colleges, collegesimply.com,* and *niche.com*. They rank schools by major, rate schools based on campus life and culture, and serve as great resources for finding potential colleges based on your field of interest.

Go explore!

College Email Account

This one tip alone may be worth the price of this book. **Create a new email account that you will use for everything college-related**. I suggest that the name of your new email account include your full last name and that you refrain from using nicknames or colloquial terms. Here are some examples of when to use this special email account:

- Applying for scholarships
- Registering for the ACT/SAT
- Registering for college tours
- Requesting information on a college website
- Signing up for college blogs
- Signing up for college help websites (e.g. Parchment)
- Signing up for college newsletters
- Signing up for the Common App or Coalition App

The email account used for college-related activities will get inundated with emails every day as you get closer to your senior year in high school. Personal or high school-related emails can easily be overlooked when your mailbox is flooded with college-related information. Students have missed out on opportunities because urgent or important emails have gone to the junk folder of their normal email account.

Tenth Grade—Planning for the "Next"

You must be committed to working the plan toward your goals!

"Tomorrow belongs to the people who prepare for it today"
–African proverb

Note: If this is the first chapter that you are reading in this book, I highly recommend that you go back and read the preceding chapters before continuing. Doing so will allow you to take full advantage of the information presented in the chapters that follow. Know that you might have work to do to catch up on things you may have missed, but do not worry; you still have time!

Sophomore year requires that you adopt a mindset centered around establishing your ideal college application profile. You will need to be purposeful about taking the necessary actions to accomplish the milestones you have set to fulfill your vision.

This chapter is a model for the sophomore year wheel needed to drive off towards college success. Our objective is to:

» Continue to comprehend the importance of **reading regularly** and **ACT/SAT prep**
» Take on responsibility for your results through the **accountability transition**

» Integrate the final elements of good **discipline: focus on perseverance** and **consistency**
» Fully understand the decision process for taking **college prep courses**
» Perform action items towards building your ideal college admissions profile:
  › Focus on your mental health
  › Begin to look for leadership opportunities
  › Research programs and activities for the upcoming summer
  › Create a spreadsheet to track colleges of interest
  › Create a spreadsheet to track scholarships of interest
  › Research majors offered by specific colleges
  › Continue your ACT/SAT prep
  › Build your essay writing skills
  › Research resources on college applications and scholarships
  › Start your college scholarship search
  › Start planning for college tours
  › Build your high school resume
  › Clean up your social media footprint

Sophomore Focus Point: You are still reading this book, which means you have decided to take ownership of your educational career. Great! Your success in the classroom lays the groundwork for a successful high school career, so now it is time to build on that foundation by planning towards your "next." For some students, high school can be a ball of stress due to a ton of activities and worry. For others, it can be all fun with no attention paid to the future. Sometimes we focus so much on reaching milestones we have set that we miss out on enjoying ourselves during the journey. So let's make it a perfect balance of both.

Tenth Grade—Planning for the "Next"

The tenth grade is when you must start building your resumé content. You will begin filling out your college applications at the very start of your senior year, which means that the accomplishments you include will come from your first three years of high school. While some will come from freshman year, **the bulk of the meaningful accomplishments that you will list on your applications will occur in your sophomore and junior years.**

"I am who I am today because of the choices I made yesterday."
–Eleanor Roosevelt

You have high ambitions for your future, and I believe you are capable of achieving them. But there is no room for complacency! This is the time when many of your peers are slacking off, so seize your opportunity to distance yourself from them academically. Think of the dreams you have for yourself and the difference you might want to make in this world. Now ask yourself if that person you see in the future will exist if you are not willing to put in the work today? Just do not confuse commitment and hard work with overwhelming yourself with too many activities.

It is important for your mental health to navigate the delicate balance between pushing yourself and eliminating stress. Try to focus on quality over quantity when it comes to the activities you participate in: your time should be reserved for the thing(s) you are passionate about. Consider the purpose of your participation in any educational extracurricular activity or community involvement. If it does not allow you to serve others, does not have special personal meaning, or does not meet an objective in your plan, you need to reconsider the value from participating. Also, while having time set aside for fun and relaxation is an important aspect of mental health, you cannot allow fun and relaxation to dominate your time. The secret is to do what you enjoy the most, but in predefined time frames.

Cars come with a regular maintenance schedule to ensure they

Before The Application

continue to run in top condition. These checkups are designed to prevent breakdowns and correct minor issues before they become major issues. A thorough checkup can discover a potential problem before the customer ever recognizes it. This same value holds true when doing regular mental health checkups. Checking in with a parent or someone else who has your best interest at heart may be the preventive medicine you need to avoid any serious issues.

Julia Says

As you continue your journey of self-discovery, you should apply what you have learned from freshman year to your sophomore year. By now, you should have a pretty good idea of what works best for you when it comes to managing your schoolwork and your mental health. Do not worry if you do not have it down pat yet; there is still plenty of time for self-discovery. Now that you are a sophomore, start focusing on discovering yourself in the extracurricular activities department.

Now, I understand that you may want to devote all of your time to schoolwork and summer programs and that is fine and dandy, but finding the time to do what you love is essential to your mental wellness. I made the mistake of being so focused on getting straight As and having a high SAT score that I overlooked doing what would have made me happy. I did what I thought I was supposed to do, and not necessarily what I wanted to do.

My advice is to go out and explore what the world has to offer outside of the classroom. Whether it is reading a book or making a painting, the activity you choose should make you feel like you are resetting yourself and your mind. Not having that stress will make you a more productive person, because your mental state and your emotions will be at peace. In the long run, doing what you love will benefit your mental wellness. Plus, it will give you a sense of direction for the next three years so that you are not doing activities randomly. This step of self-discovery is great not only for your wellness, but also for your college applications, as colleges like being able to see that you are passionate and dedicated to something, whether it is big or small.

The Fundamentals—Building on the Foundation

Reading and ACT/SAT prep continue to be critical components.

Reading for Fun

If you already enjoy reading, GREAT! If you are like I was at your age and would rather play in poison ivy than read a book, I understand. Unfortunately, *not* reading comes with consequences. If you are not great at reading comprehension, avoiding reading is not going to make you any better at it.

I likely had undiagnosed attention deficit disorder (ADD) when I was younger, so my mind would wander off into a fantasy world as I was reading. After ten minutes, I would find myself several pages later with no idea of what I just read. I had to learn to read in 5-minute intervals and eventually worked my way up to about 30 minutes before needing to take a break. Unfortunately, I was an adult by the time I utilized this method, which means I suffered the consequences for many years. Despite my ability, I missed out on opportunities because I seemed like a less capable person than my peers simply because of subpar reading skills. I encourage you to find your pathway to reading right away so that you can begin to reap the benefits as soon as possible.

Continuous reading can be your life's ongoing teacher because information leads to knowledge, and as the old adage goes, "knowledge is power." Consider the following excerpt from the editorial "Here's How Many Books the Average CEO Reads Yearly — And What They're Reading" on Fairy God Boss, by Kayla Heisler:

> "What does it take to be number one? A recent survey by Fast Company suggests that the answer could be a well-lined bookshelf. In fact, the average number of books read by a CEO is 60 books per year, or five books each month.
>
> 'What I know for sure is that reading opens you up,' says Oprah, 'It exposes you and gives you access to anything your mind can hold. What I love most about reading—It gives you the ability to reach higher ground.'
>
> Warren Buffett is another confirmed bibliophile, who reportedly reads an astounding average of 500 pages each day! Buffett attributes his success partly to his voracious reading habit and encourages others to incorporate reading into their daily routine, saying: 'Read 500 pages like this every day. That's how knowledge works. It builds up, like compound interest.'"

Reading Check-In!

Did you complete your reading challenge?

I was able to finish _____ books over the last year.

Just like last year, you should accept the **Commitment to Reading Challenge** over the next year by picking the option that best fits you. For example, challenge yourself to read one book per month or for at least two hours per week.

I *will* read a minimum of _____ books over the next year.

–OR–

I *will* read a minimum of _____ hours per week over the next year.

For suggestions on reading material, you can still refer to the Helen Ruffin Reading Bowl Booklist and follow Project Lit on social media for age appropriate book ideas. In addition to these are great resources, this year I would like to share with you the favorite book from each of my boys when they were in high school:

- » **Christopher**—*Monster* by Walter Dan Meyers
- » **Brian**—*An Absolutely Remarkable Thing* by Hank Green (and its sequel, *A Beautifully Foolish Endeavor*)
- » **Aaron**—*The Ranger's Apprentice* by John Flanagan (series) and *The Giver* by Lois Lowry

You can also visit my website at *woolfolkworks.com/readinglist* for my sons' Top 10 Reading List and book recommendations shared by readers of this book just like you.

ACT/SAT Prep

When it comes to ACT/SAT prep, there is great value in exposure and repetition. The reward of a strong score is worth the effort you put into practicing now. Take professional athletes for example. We see them perform at a high level on game day, and they manage to make it look easy. Chris Morris, a close friend of mine, was the fourth overall pick in the NBA draft and played in the league for thirteen years. Three of those years were spent with the Utah Jazz where he played head-to-head against Michael Jordan during the Bulls' final two championship runs.

Before The Application

I saw firsthand the *thousands* of hours of practice and training that were critical for him to achieve this level of success.

The same can be seen with professional dancers. I am a big fan of dance, and I enjoy watching a strong dance company perform, especially the Alvin Ailey American Dance Theater. The elegance and power demonstrated on that stage is astounding. These women and men have been dancing all their lives through many injuries and obstacles. They spend hundreds of hours in rehearsal for a flawless two-hour performance on stage.

Similarly, in order to look back and be proud of your performance, you must first look forward and prepare for your desired results. During your sophomore year:

» Continue (or start) doing at least one ACT/SAT question each day. Do your best to work your way towards the correct answer. When you check your answer, be sure to look for the skill the questions were testing for and the method used to derive the answer. If the skill is not one that you are familiar with, add it to the list of skills you need to brush up on.

» Every other weekend or so, take one practice test section and time yourself. It is important to get a feel for answering the questions in a timely manner. Like the ACT/SAT question of the day, analyze the results for both the right and wrong answers. Never assume that you used the best approach just because you ended up with the correct answer, as it may not be time efficient.

» Have your parent (or someone else) assist with your ACT/SAT prep. Remember that the most important question in education is "Why?" With either the question of the day or the practice test, have your parent look at the correct answer while you explain to them *why* you chose your answer. There is merit in explaining your answer to someone out loud.

» Choose the timeline for when you will take the official SAT or ACT. There are differing lines of thinking regarding how often a student should take these tests. I have already stated that my kids took the October test during their freshman and sophomore years at the same location they would take the test their junior and senior years. This way, they were comfortable with their testing location by eleventh grade.

Some would argue that the official test should not be taken that early or often. If you subscribe to this philosophy, choose one of the official testing dates and simulate the actual test scenario by taking the entire test in the proper timed fashion and then self-score it for your results. We chose to take the test in October because this was the latest reasonable date that allowed us to meet early college application deadlines during senior year. There are people who strongly feel that there is an advantage to taking the test in late spring of junior year. Do your research and follow a plan that feels most comfortable to you.

ACT/SAT Score Tracker

It is time to record any new scores from over the past year and track the progress you have made. Doing so will let you know if you are on the right pace or if you may need to improve your prep strategy. Remember that if testing independently, you can estimate your score by using the Raw Score Conversion Table on College Board's website or the Sample ACT Scoring Chart on The Princeton Review's website.

Sophomore Essentials—Taking Control

The Accountability Transition

Accountability answers the question of who is the single person that will take responsibility for the consequences for one's actions. During most of my talks, I typically ask, "Who is responsible for the education of a child?" I hear a variety of answers, but most often I receive the response, "The parent." It is important for parents to focus on their role in education, which includes partnering with the school and supplementing their child's education where necessary.

However, determining ownership of accountability depends on when the question is asked, so the balance between you and your parent should follow a natural progression. At a young age, a child is not mature enough to have accountability for their education. Starting in middle school, accountability should shift to be shared between parent and student. Ideally, by sophomore year, the shift should be nearly complete. By the end of the school year, you ought to have full accountability for your education, with your parent assisting by holding you accountable to your responsibilities.

The graduation rates at colleges are alarmingly low—according to *educationdata.org*, only 41% of students graduate from a 4-year college within 4 years. If colleges only accept students that are capable of successfully graduating, why is it that 4 out of 10 students do not graduate? The Education Advisory Board (*eab.com*) addressed the "7 Reasons—Other than Cost—That Students Don't Graduate." Three of those reasons can be attributed to the fact that students are going off to college with no experience in being accountable for their own actions. Below, you will find the seven reasons along with key points from chapters in this book that would proactively address each one:

Tenth Grade—Planning for the "Next"

1. They're juggling work and school → **Organization and Time Management**
2. No one told them how many credits to take → **Accountability**
3. They transferred schools, but their credits didn't come with them → **Accountability**
4. They fell into the "exploration" trap → **College Major Research**
5. They got stuck in remedial courses → **Everything You Do Matters** and **A Mindset of Excellence**
6. They lack confidence → **Grit**
7. They couldn't navigate the hidden curriculum → **Accountability**

In the Ownership section of the Freshman chapter I revealed that knowing your "why" provides value to your education, which should serve as motivation for achieving your plan. Accountability is more about your "*how*," because as you accept sole responsibility for the consequences of your actions, you will approach everything you do in a manner of excellence. **When it comes to your education, the one and only person that is truly impacted by your decisions is you**.

It is disheartening when students struggle in college because their parent did everything for them their entire lives. As you begin to take *full* accountability for your education, here are a few ideas for tackling this transition:

- » Build a *relationship* of trust with your teachers.
- » Go to school for the purpose of learning, not just performing for a grade.
- » Have a *mindset of excellence* and remember that *everything you do matters.*
- » Strengthen your *discipline* by focusing on its five elements: motivation, time management, organization, perseverance, and consistency.
- » Take *responsibility* for your own problems and issues.

> » Update your *plan* which includes your vision and the necessary goals to achieve it.

One of the worst parts of a student dropping out of college is the financial debt incurred with nothing to show for it. Not being able to finish your degree is just like making payments on a car that you are not allowed to take home from the dealership. Thankfully, I did not have to drop out of college, but it did take me six years and attending three different colleges to earn my degree. Just as I was determined to prevent my kids from having this struggle, I want to do the same for you.

The Accountability Transition—Parents

Parents, you have a role in helping your child learn to be accountable for their work and their actions. Start by allowing them to have more control of their lives and deal with their issues directly. **This is not the same as taking a completely hands-off approach**. You should still be there as a guide who provides advice along the way. Asking them the questions that they should be asking themselves is the best way to help them learn accountability. A few examples are:

> » Do you have any assignments missing?
> » Do you understand the consequences of your decision?
> » Have you set reminders for action items that need to be done at regular intervals?
> » How often do you review your listed grades to confirm they were logged correctly?
> » How would you approach a teacher to discuss a problem or address a disagreement?
> » What is your plan for completing your research paper/essay/major assignments?
> » (I would suggest scheduling checkpoints to review their progress.)

Before the school year starts, you and your child should settle on the consequences for failing to meet an agreed upon standard of excellence for their schoolwork. Over the course of the year, check your child's gradebook for assignments you suspect may not demonstrate their best effort. Discuss the circumstances that may have affected their performance to determine if consequences are warranted. It is important to teach your child how to be accountable and accept the consequences of their actions, both good and bad.

Discipline—Focus on Perseverance

The fourth "Element of Discipline" is perseverance. This element is a major part of grit, which was discussed near the beginning of the book. Let's explore this topic a little more in depth. **Perseverance is all about creating a mindset for success**. Consider the following example:

"I got to go study for a test."
vs.
"I get to go study for a test."

Perseverance starts with an appreciation for the opportunities you have today. Instead of complaining about the many things we *have* to do on a daily basis, begin to appreciate the privilege of having these tasks. This simple adjustment from an "o" to an "e" demonstrates your gratitude for receiving an education that affords you an opportunity to become a self-sufficient adult. An appreciation for your current opportunities can become the driving force that pushes you to confidently seize the opportunities that await you.

"I want to get a Bachelor of Science in Nursing."
vs.
"I will get a Bachelor of Science in Nursing."

Okay, okay, I know this is more than a one-letter change but let us focus on migrating from an attitude of "want" to an attitude of "will." A nursing degree is a great goal to have, but what happens when obstacles fall into your path? What will you do if your dream college does not accept you, or you get that one professor that fails half the class, or you do not have a job offer before you graduate college? Perseverance is all about grit, which builds determination and strength to overcome adversity. Times will get tough and things will not always go according to plan. The question is, will you use your grit to generate an attitude of determination to overcome your obstacles? When you merely "want" to do something, you can be easily deterred, especially when it is inconvenient. When you "will" do something, you take responsibility and have the determination to see it through. **Perseverance requires the discipline to stay focused, as well as a resilient belief in yourself and an understanding that some level of sacrifice will be necessary**.

No matter your circumstances, grit is the gasoline that will continue to propel your car forward. This applies whether you have that one subject that you struggle with or if you are a "naturally gifted" student in high school who may stumble only when facing bigger challenges in college. You can build your grit by always putting forth your best effort utilizing the concept that everything you do matters and developing a mindset of excellence.

> **Parents:** Your role here is to build up your student. Your child constantly hears comments from you that they perceive to be negative, even though it is usually for their own good. Sometimes they need to hear that you believe in them. Let them know that the reason you challenge them is because you know that greatness is in their future. Most people need someone to believe in them before they can believe in themselves! This instilled confidence combined with appreciation results in a passionate determination.

College Prep Courses— Choosing Wisely

In general, college prep courses are designed to meet the minimum course requirements that many colleges have for admission. They are offered at varying levels of difficulty, each designed to better prepare students for the rigors of college. You *may* have the opportunity to choose between a variety of pathways: On-Level, Honors/Advanced, Dual Enrollment, Advanced Placement (AP), and International Baccalaureate (IB) Diploma Programme (DP). There is no one "right" answer, but there is a "best fit" for each student. Making the best decision on college prep courses is directly related to your ability and the types of colleges you aspire to attend. This is another reason why reviewing college websites at an early stage is important. Families often do not realize the impact this decision has on college acceptances until it is too late.

Special Note: As this section involves course scheduling, I need to stress an important concern about interacting with your professional school counselor. During the early part of the next chapter, I will discuss the importance of maintaining positive relationships with your teachers and counselor. Before this time, you may have to work with your counselor to resolve an issue. **Do not cause a rift between you and your counselor because your interactions will leave a lasting impression and they *will* have influence on your college applications.**

This section is a bit lengthy but contains vital information, so bear with me. I will answer the following questions:

1. What do I mean by your "ability" to handle one of the college prep pathways?
2. What are the typical class options for college-bound students? What are the pros and cons of each?

3. Why must you consider your potential college application pool before making this decision?
4. What else should you consider before making this call?

Your "ability" is not just your aptitude

All options for a college prep pathway have a certain level of difficulty and require a certain demand on your time. The degree to which these factors come into play will be affected by how your school implements each program. Therefore, you must determine ahead of time your ability to commit to a pathway based on several components. This includes whether you:

- » are a slow or a fast reader
- » are able to grasp concepts during class or require after school tutorial
- » have demands on your time from extracurricular activities
- » have the ability to grasp difficult concepts
- » need to review material when studying for exams often
- » need to study more or less than the average student
- » perform well on major exams or struggle with test anxiety
- » require a significant amount of time to complete homework

Typical class options for college-bound students

I encourage you to do your own research to better understand your options, but here is my perspective on the different programs:

- » <u>On-level Classes</u>—These are standard classes typically offered to the majority of students within a school.

Pros:
> - Meets the minimum course load requirements needed for admissions at many colleges.
> - Will not overburden students who are not ready for the challenges that come with higher level college prep programs

Cons:
> - Lack of rigor will count against students at most colleges for admissions
> - Does not qualify for college credit
> - Will not be an indicator for students' potential to be successful in college

» Honors or Advanced Classes—Typically, these are challenging courses that are not governed by a national or international board, so they may go by different titles. The curriculum is typically identical to on-level, but Honors courses should have an internal expectation of rigor governed by the school/district's policies. The true level of rigor in a course is determined by the quality of the school and teacher.

Pros:
> - Best fit for students that need to be challenged without the pressure and rigor that come with college-level courses
> - A decent measure to determine if a student will be ready for the rigors of college
> - High schools may offer points to boost final grade
> - May be most ideal for students who want an academic challenge but have other heavy demands on their time

Cons:
> - Does not qualify for college credit
> - Will count against students at many colleges when more rigorous courses are offered at the school

Before The Application

- » Dual Enrollment—These are courses that a student takes at an accredited college for high school credit, either in person or online.

  Pros:
  - › Has the potential to qualify for college credit
  - › Provides a great introduction to a college learning atmosphere
  - › Can serve as the highest available rigor if a high school does not offer AP or IB courses
  - › High schools may offer points to boost final grade

  Cons:
  - › College atmosphere comes with college-level grading (you cannot expect final grades to be boosted or saved by homework assignments, quizzes, and in-class participation)
  - › Full accountability is placed on the student without handholding (some students are not mature enough to handle this)
  - › Less access to professors (time conflicts due to high school schedule)
  - › Can be a waste of time without the understanding of how credits will transfer to target colleges
  - › May lack camaraderie with college classmates who do not bond with high school students
  - › May miss out on some experiences by being out of the school building such as class meetings, college visits, impromptu announcements, and intangibles like the benefit of a true senior experience and making lifetime memories

- » Advanced Placement (AP)—These are courses governed by the College Board (the same organization that administers the SAT). Due to the AP assessment exams being national, they can be used by colleges to gauge how students across the country compare to one another.

Pros:
› Provides more in-depth and challenging courses of college-like rigor
› Widely accepted at most colleges and universities for college credit
› AP schedule can be customized towards subjects a student excels in
› Most high schools offer additional points to final grade to compensate for the higher rigor (possibly more points than Honors/Advanced courses)

Cons:
› Some students may struggle with these more intense courses
› Cost of about $100 for the end-of-course AP exam (some schools may cover this cost)
› Courses appear to be more content-based versus application-based
› College credit is based on your score from a single exam taken at the end of the school year (grade in course has no impact on credit)
› Can become too focused on test preparation alone
› Even when adequately focused on test prep, some schools still do a poor job of preparing students to pass the test, which works against students who wish to attain college credit

» International Baccalaureate (IB) Diploma Programme (DP)— This is a sanctioned, international program that offers a variety of curricula from elementary through high school. At the high school level, you can opt to be a full IB Diploma Candidate or select any number of DP courses where you will receive a certificate for successful performance on the IB assessments. Courses are offered at two levels: Higher Level (HL) and

Standard Level (SL). The difference between the two is the amount of content covered, as well as possibly an additional paper when you sit for your official IB assessments. HL courses will be more in-depth and hold you to a higher standard on your External and Internal Assessment (IA). I highly recommend visiting *ibo.org/parents* for more information.

Pros:
- A very rigorous program designed to delve into the breadth and depth of all subjects offered
- A collective body of work that spans two years versus an independent set of courses
- Focuses on learning and application rather than concentrating on the end-of-course test
- Earning the diploma involves a holistic approach that entails more than just final subject exams
- Prepares a student to be a college-level learner
- Taking DP courses for a certificate allows students to be selective of which IB courses they wish to pursue by subject (the overall rigor can be better managed)

Cons:
- Very rigorous and time-consuming (should be chosen only by students who can handle the demands, as they can easily become overwhelming)
- Difficult to manage with competing activities that require a demand on time (also likely to put a damper on a student's social life)
- High schools are usually limited in their ability to offer both HL and SL courses
- Not offered by all school districts but becoming more widely known and respected
- Some colleges only give credit for Higher Level (HL) courses

Consider your potential college application pool before making a decision

I will now further explain why the decision you make has a direct bearing on your chances for college acceptances in the future. Unfortunately, too many students do not learn this lesson until they become seniors and start the application process, which is usually too late to take corrective action.

If Ivy League institutions or Ivy League competitors are in your pool of potential colleges, they will want to see that you took the absolute most rigorous group of classes offered by your school. If your school does not offer enough rigor, they will want to see you take advantage of programs like dual enrollment. The core classes on your transcript (along with AP exam scores, if applicable) will likely have a strong bearing on your admissions decision. Again, not every college is the same and at some schools, an outstanding overall application may overcome a less than stellar performance in these areas.

Therefore, it is important to have a general idea of the student profile for the colleges you wish to apply to. A college student profile is my term for what a particular college deems to be important for the brand of student they primarily like to recruit. Fitting into this brand helps make students competitive for a school, yet *how* a student fits this profile should be unique and genuine. A technical school may prefer a student that demonstrates a commitment to STEM-related academic excellence, while a small liberal arts college may focus on students that demonstrate a commitment to social issues. The student profile for Stanford is completely different from the student profile for Harvard, just like the student profile for Vanderbilt is completely different from the student profile for UC Berkeley.

The need to take a rigorous course load is not limited to the top private schools in the country. Top state schools and competitive private schools want to see rigor as well. These schools tend to be a bit more lenient on whether you are taking the absolute most rigorous set of courses, but they still want to see a transcript full of challenging courses. Again, you must understand the student profile for the school you are targeting. I have seen the requirements to attend the University of Georgia (UGA) drastically change in the last twenty years. I know of a parent who had their child dual enroll in Algebra I as a junior. This was sufficient for the parent to be accepted to UGA twenty-five years ago, but their child had no chance of admission because they did not fit UGA's current student profile.

I do not want to leave the impression that all college-bound students must enroll in the toughest classes their school offers. There are plenty of good colleges that do not require such a high level of rigor. However, this does not diminish the need to match your pathway with the style of school you wish to attend. In the other direction, assessing your ability and deciding on your college prep pathway may help you choose your pool of potential college choices.

Things to consider before making your decision

AP versus IB—People often wonder which of these two programs is better. There is no clear answer, but here are some items for consideration when making the choice for yourself:

- » Some colleges give more weight to one program over the other, so if your priority is to get as much college credit as possible, review the requirements for receiving credit at any college(s) you are interested in attending. Remember to check whether they give credit for IB Standard Level (SL) courses.
- » Only consider IB Diploma if you are ready to make the commitment; otherwise, consider the flexibility of taking AP courses and/or pursuing IB certificates. At the same time, do not let the amount of work deter you from the IB Diploma Programme, as it is a great preamble to college.
- » Compare the track record of the AP versus IB teachers within your school.

» If you have participated in the IB Middle Years Programme (MYP), you are in a much better position to handle the IB Diploma Programme, but I still caution you to weigh the decision carefully due to the many demands that are required to be met.
» As always, I encourage you to conduct your own independent research regarding which program is best for you.

Consider Being Creative—There are no rules that say you cannot put together a plan that includes a mixture of courses from more than one pathway. I worked with one young lady who took two IB courses but recognized that her high school performed very poorly on the IB exam in another subject that would be part of her intended major in college. Therefore, she took that course at a local college after assuring she would receive the college credit at her desired school.

Personalize the Program—Do NOT put pressure on yourself to take every single one of the most rigorous courses offered at your school. You do not have to take five AP courses at one time or enter the full IB Diploma Programme (unless you can handle it and you are targeting top schools). **Based on your anticipated target and stretch schools, design a personalized program that fits your talents and abilities**. Colleges want to see that you took challenging courses related to your intended major. For example, if you plan to major in engineering, schools want to see that you took the most challenging math and physics courses available to you. The fact that not all of your core classes are being taken at the highest level of rigor does not mean that you can slack off as most colleges still want to see some level of rigor in all remaining core classes.

Individualize the Program—Your college prep pathway should be based on your unique ability to handle rigor, the expectations of your anticipated target colleges, and your desire to increase your college readiness. For this reason, I caution you to not choose your pathway based on the success of another student or sibling or just because it is popular at your school. Just like Goldilocks, you want to find the fit that is "just right."

College Credit—If earning college credit is an important goal of your college prep pathway, you must find out what credits are accepted by your pool of potential colleges. If you dual enroll with a college, make sure your target schools will accept credits from that college and that the specific courses you are taking will transfer. If you are going the route of AP or IB, understand that you should balance the need to take rigorous courses with the risk of not passing the exam to receive credit. Also be aware that colleges have different minimum score requirements for assessment exams in order to receive credit.

College Credit Caution—The opportunity for college credit should not be the primary reason for selecting your college prep pathway because it is not always wise to automatically use all of your earned college credit. Some students are better served by waiting to take the first level of a course once they get to college in order to adjust to that school's rigor and style. The student I referred to above (who created her own pathway) received credit for Calculus 1 based on her participation in Dual Enrollment. She ended up struggling in Calculus 2 during her freshman year because the college where she took the course during high school taught at a slower pace than the college that she eventually attended. I also suggest that any course that serves as a prerequisite for higher level courses should be considered extra carefully, especially if it is within the discipline of your chosen major. Those who do extremely well on the end-of-course AP/IB exams are typically prepared to apply the credit. Regardless, a student needs to make this decision independently for every course where they have earned credit.

GPA versus Rigor—One reason some students shy away from the AP and IB pathways is the potential negative impact on their GPA, yet many colleges prefer seeing the challenging course load on a transcript over a top 5 class ranking. If your target schools require the rigor offered by AP and IB courses and you believe you are up for the challenge, the benefits will likely be worth it. This is especially true considering how well these courses prepare you to be college ready.

Scholarships—Most colleges offer scholarships ranging from a few hundred dollars all the way up to full tuition or a full ride. I strongly believe that AP and IB pathways give students a better chance of winning the bigger scholarships. From the sample of colleges our family has been involved with, the profile of the students that receive these scholarships tend to include a strong presence of AP or IB courses (or sometimes dual enrollment from highly respected colleges).

Making the decision

Be wise when deciding between On-Level, Honors/Advanced, Dual Enrollment, AP, IB Diploma, IB Certificate, or your own combination. Be honest when evaluating your ability, your desire to take ownership of your education, and your willingness to be accountable for your choices. I discourage overburdening yourself in high school equally as much as taking too light of a load. This decision must be made with an understanding of the level of competitiveness for schools you are targeting. Placing yourself in the best college prep program does not mean choosing the level that is easy for you, but rather choosing an environment that adequately challenges you. If you are not willing to challenge yourself in high school, then you are not building the proper mindset to be successful in college. I strongly encourage that this be a family decision.

> **Parents**: You do not want to put your child into a situation beyond their capabilities, but you also do not want to stunt their growth by not challenging them. Find this balance by examining who you both believe they can grow into instead

of limiting them to who they were in the past, who they are now, or an impression of who they can become based on your personal experiences. *Without a doubt, you MUST have the "buy in" from your child as this decision is made.*

In our house, I helped my children do the research to determine the pros and cons, gave my honest assessment of their potential, and then told them which pathway I felt was best for them. But at the end of the day, I allowed them to make the decision. This made it easy to remind them that it was *their* call and to hold them accountable to their path.

Sophomore Timeline— Generating Momentum

THANKSGIVING BREAK

Evaluation Time

Just as you did during your freshman year, take some time before your Thanksgiving break to evaluate how classes are progressing. Have an honest conversation with your parent or someone you trust to determine if there are any areas where you may be struggling. Whether in high school, in college, in the workplace, or in your personal life—***when you need help, ask for it***!

How have you been doing with balance in your life? I have placed a lot of emphasis on a mindset of excellence and believing that everything you do matters. Developing these attributes will have a big impact on your drive to be successful, but remember to keep an eye on your mental health. As you go forward with the rest of your sophomore year, be sure to challenge yourself AND find an outlet to release your stress. Whenever you need to, please take the time to go back and read the sections on mental health. During this break, schedule a check-in with a parent or another adult you respect and have an open conversation about what you are going through. Having these chats on a regular basis will help you maintain your all-important mental health in the long run. Your concerns do not have to be considered big by the world for them to be big to you.

Leadership Opportunities

Freshman year was about exploring opportunities for leadership and joining organizations with future leadership possibilities. Remember that in the fall of your senior year you will be writing about your leadership experiences on applications. This means you must gain these experiences during sophomore and junior years. While there should be several prospects in clubs or organizations within and outside of your school, you cannot expect to just show up the first year and be elected president. It is not too late to join an organization that interests you in order to place yourself in a position for a leadership role next year. If you are already a member of an organization from freshman year, sophomore year is a great time to take a lower leadership role that you can use for experience when running for a higher position the following year. Even if you do not hold the title of president (though it is a nice visual on your application), you can still effect change from another position or as just a member. Also, remember that you have the ability to create your own leadership opportunities!

Leadership is not dependent on organizations or fancy titles. Remember that leadership can be combined with Community Service or Demonstrated Passion/Strong Interest. Think along the lines of:

» Creating a tutoring service where you get the math/science/reading club to volunteer at local middle schools for free tutoring one day a week.
» Creating an event similar to a career fair where professionals amongst parents and the local community set up stations, and students can learn about various career options.

Be creative! **Remember, the best ideas come from identifying a problem and building an effective program to address it.**

CHRISTMAS BREAK

Research Summer Programs

I have encouraged your participation in summer programs in areas like leadership, academic research, arts, STEM (robotics, coding, game design), social issues, music, etc. This will benefit you as you learn more about potential college majors or career fields and when you are eventually filling out college applications. If available to you, consider participating in one of these types of programs held on a college campus and/or as a residential program. The added benefit of attending a program on a college campus is gaining exposure to a college atmosphere. The value in participating in overnight programs (even if they are not focused on learning) is that you can experience what it is like to be away from your family for an extended period of time before you first go off to college. It is good to have a taste of personal responsibility, and summer programs are a great way to accomplish this.

As a reminder, now is the time to look for summer programs as the free and less expensive ones tend to fill up quickly. Take note of application deadlines, any associated costs, and requirements for acceptance. You may also want to take this time to look for weekend programs in your field of interest that take place during the school year (if you can fit them into your schedule).

SPRING BREAK

College Tracking Spreadsheet

It is common for admissions officers from four to five different colleges or universities to hold informational group sessions in various cities across the country, and my son Brian and I attended one of these expos. Before they started their school-specific presentations, each admissions officer shared their best tips for students applying to any college. The very first piece of advice given was to create a spreadsheet that lists every college you are interested in attending along with likes, dislikes, and any details you learn about the school. The admissions officer explained that the college search process can be overwhelming, and it is easy to forget details about schools you researched, learned about or visited early in the process. My son looked over at me and then at my iPad with our version of the spreadsheet* open before shaking his head in surrender. I did not even have to say, "I told you so."

I encourage you to find a way to physically or digitally track information about the colleges you visit in person or virtually. Let's do a quick calculation of how many things you will need to keep track of over a span of several months when applying to colleges. The recommended number of colleges that a high school student is encouraged to apply to is between 6 and 8 (Prep Scholar), up to a maximum of 12 to 15 (Ivywise & Forbes). The average number of colleges that students actually apply to is between 7 and 10 (College Vine). There will be at least 20 pieces of information you will need to compile for each college you apply to, plus 4 to 5 other details I suggest you document. This adds up to over *200* items that you will need to track for completion, all while handling the busyness that comes with being a high school senior.

I believe that one of the leading factors as to why students miss out on attending their desired schools is a lack of organization that leads to missed deadlines and subpar applications. It hurts my heart that one of the young ladies that graduated with my youngest son was accepted to her dream school, the University of Virginia (arguably the number one public university in the nation), but she missed the financial aid deadline, which prohibited her from attending the college.

Now is the best time to create your document to record all the necessary tracking items for your potential colleges. Having something like this in place is *vital* when applying to colleges during your senior year. I suggest

Before The Application

using a spreadsheet but feel free to use any format that you are comfortable with. For each college you research, you will list all necessary application information and their requirements along with due dates. During your senior year, you will mark each item as complete as you submit it.

Here is a list of suggested items to include in your document:

College Name	Link to website
Regular or Early application?	App deadline(s)
Application cost	Accept Common or Coalition app?
Link to scholarships & deadlines	Financial aid deadline
CSS Profile required for financial aid?	Transcript
Self-report ACT/SAT?	Superscore ACT/SAT?
Teacher recommendations, how many?	Teacher recommendations, specified teacher?
Counselor recommendation	Optional recommendation?
Interview required or suggested?	Entrance Exam?
Midyear report	College Level: Safe/Target/Stretch
Level of interest: 1–10	Additional essays or questions?

* *A template for this spreadsheet can be purchased at woolfolkworks.com/templates or you may wish to use our dedicated app College Tracker, which can also be found on the website.*

Once the spreadsheet is created, choose one college you will almost certainly apply to and do the research to fill out the spreadsheet. Here is a snippet from my middle son Brian's spreadsheet at the end of the application process. We used color coding to track items and checkmarks to denote when the entire application was complete. You can see that he listed one school (Princeton) he later determined he would not apply to.

Tenth Grade—Planning for the "Next"

College	Deadline	Scholarships	SAT/ACT	Super-score	Subject Test	Essay	App Cost	Teacher Recom	Common Skol Rprt	Common Colg App
Harvard ✓ https://college.harvard.edu/admissions	11/15/16 Regular		Both		Yes 2		$75	Yes 2	Yes w/ Recom	Yes
Yale ✓ https://admissions.yale.edu/	12/15/16 Regular			Yes	Recom	Yes	$80	Yes 2	Yes w/ Recom	Yes
Princeton ✓ https://admissions.princeton.edu/	12/15/16 (but they encourage by Dec 15)			N/A	Recom 2		$65	Yes 2	Yes w/ Recom	
Stanford ✓ https://admissions.stanford.edu/	11/15/16 Regular		Both	Yes	Recom 1	Yes	$90	Yes 2	Yes w/ Recom	Yes
Vanderbilt ✓ https://admissions.vanderbilt.edu/	11/15/16 Regular	Cornelius, Chancellor https://vanderbilt.edu/scholars	Both	Yes	Yes 2		$50	Yes 2	Recom	Yes
Rice https://futureowls.rice.edu/home.aspx	11/15/16 Regular	Yes, but automatic application	Both	Yes	Yes 2	Yes	$75	Yes 1	Yes w/ Recom	Yes

107

Before The Application

This exercise will give you the proper respect for the work behind applying to college and a great head start over your peers. As an added bonus, this work will provide perspective to why you are reading this book and the importance of preparing early in your high school career.

Scholarship Tracking Spreadsheet

Take the time to create another spreadsheet* for potential scholarships. It is amazing how often we hear about the need for money, yet most students do not take the time to apply for independent scholarships. It may take applying to 30 scholarships just to receive one, but every dollar earned now could save from you paying double that amount in college debt. There are also some obscure scholarships that do not get many applicants, so you will have a higher chance of winning one just by applying. The leading reasons that students do not take the time to apply for scholarships comes down to laziness, busyness, or a lack of organization.

Every year I read about a few students who received multiple independent scholarships, and I have discovered two major drivers behind their success that share a common denominator: these students apply to a large number of scholarships and they have that "WOW" factor in their high school resumé. The "WOW" factor could come from the great volunteer work they have done, or maybe from an organization they started, or possibly from their solution to a unique problem in their community. Successful students are able to implement these factors to win scholarships through their mastery of the **Elements of Discipline**.

Although it may not be time to populate it, I suggest building your scholarship document now. Again, I prefer using a spreadsheet, but you should go with your preference. This one is much simpler as there are fewer details to cover:

Tenth Grade—Planning for the "Next"

Name of Scholarship	Website link
Amount	Renewable (Y/N)
Opening date	Closing date
Requirements	Eligibility

* *A template for this spreadsheet can be downloaded for free at woolfolkworks.com/templates*

Here is a sample from Brian's scholarship spreadsheet:

Scholarship Name	Amount	Renew	Deadline	Eligibility	Essay and Other Requirements
Delta Community Credit Union Scholarship	$5,000	No	04/01/17	3.0 GPA, DCCU Member	Essay: 300–500 words, transcript, acceptance letter
Coco-Cola Scholars Foundation Scholarship	$20,000	No	10/31/16		Transcript, activities, awards
Burger King Scholars Program	$1,000–$50,000	No	12/31/16	2.5 GPA, 1st 50,000 applicants	Work/activities, transcript
Bryan Cameron Foundation	$20,000–$50,000	No	09/15/16	307 GPA, demonstrated passion, leadership, and community service	Transcript, 2 letters of recommendation

I encourage you to begin your scholarship research now to get a running start on top of your head start of creating the scholarship spreadsheet this spring break. In fact, you can jump ahead to the College Scholarship Search section of the Sophomore Summer Timeline for some thoughts I share on the topic.

Research Majors

One of the biggest decisions you will make in your life will be choosing your college major. This decision is arguably even bigger than choosing a college! Your college degree sets you on the road for the career you will have for the majority of your adult life. Yet I have found that most students apply to colleges without a full understanding of the variety of majors offered by these institutions.

Spend a few hours searching the websites of at least five colleges to discover the many types of majors they offer. Be sure to select a variety of colleges and focus on disciplines that interest you. You want to review any intriguing minors and consider the potential of having a double major. Some schools allow a lot more flexibility in creating your own major, so you may discover the possibility of combining two passions you never thought could go together. Write down any majors that catch your attention and investigate any that were not on your radar previously. Also spend some time on a search engine looking for unique college majors. Doing all of the research mentioned in this section may open your mind up to possibilities you never would have imagined otherwise.

SUMMER BREAK

ACT/SAT Prep

Up to this point you have been doing a question per day on an app such as Daily Practice for the SAT, and you have been taking untimed practice test sections over the weekends. Remember that the road to strong scores is paved by exposure, practice, repetition, and testing strategies:

- » Exposure ensures that you run across styles of questions you have not seen before.

> » Taking practice tests ensures that you are comfortable with the flow and timing of the test.
> » Repetition ensures that you have experience answering the same type of question asked with slightly different variations. This makes you less likely to fall for tricks.
> » Utilizing proper testing strategies is the key to getting through timed tests.

I want to reiterate that most college-bound students have learned the majority of the testing content by the end of their sophomore year, so content cannot be the major determinate for a great score. Recall that a lack of reading comprehension is a detriment to test-taking abilities. Familiarity and experience with the test will eliminate a lot of the surprises that many students experience. **Preparation over time separates the *good* scores from the *great* scores.**

In math, there is usually more than one strategy to answering a question, and in writing and reading, there may be more than one approach to getting the correct answer. The simplest and most straightforward way of answering many questions typically takes the most time and will not allow you to finish a given section. This is done by design. The test is written so that a standard approach can result in a good score, but advanced thinking is required for a great score. This means you must develop different testing strategies designed to address each style of question that is presented on the exams.

You can find study books that teach good testing strategies and companies who offer excellent programs that provide even deeper insights. Every person has a different learning style. For those who can self-study effectively, utilizing a study guide should be sufficient. For students who are auditory and visual learners, there are some good online programs. There are options for students that need live interaction as well. Of course, the associated price goes up with each option. You want to make sure you choose a program with a proven history of properly teaching these strategies. My sons were fortunate to attend a high school that offered an in-school program led by Applerouth. We were incredibly pleased with their style of instruction and the techniques they taught.

This summer is the ideal time to work on test taking strategies. In addition, a lot of value is gained from taking at least one timed section each week. If you have any unanswered questions after the allotted time, finish the test by marking your remaining answers in a way that differentiates them from the ones you answered within the time limit. (Even though you are no longer being timed, still approach the remainder of the test as if you were.)

When done, use the total number of questions in the section to calculate the percentage of questions you answered correctly based on how far you got by the end of the designated time. Then, calculate the percentage of questions you got correct based on your answers for the entire section. As you do more timed practice test sections, you want to track your progress for the number of questions you are able to complete in the allotted amount of time to see if you need to work on time-saving strategies. By tracking the percent you get correct for the questions answered within time and the percent correct including the untimed questions, you can determine how much you need to focus on test question strategies.

You should also review the strategy you used to answer each question and compare it to the recommended strategy provided in the answer section of the book. Finally, keep a running list of any content that you did not know so that you can brush up on it or learn that skill.

Essay Writing

It is time for more practice leading up to your actual college application essay. Again, I want you to get accustomed to writing an essay about yourself using an actual college prompt. Your instructions are the same as last summer with new prompts:

» Choose one of the following prompts that I adapted from The Princeton Review:
   1. **Describe a problem you have solved or a problem you would like to solve.**
   2. Present a situation or quandary and show steps toward the solution. Explain how you became aware of the dilemma, how you tackled solving it, and why the problem was important to you.
   3. **Discuss an accomplishment, event, or realization that sparked a period of personal growth and a new understanding of yourself or others.**
   4. The accomplishment or event you write about can be anything from a major milestone to a smaller "Aha!" moment. Describe the event or accomplishment that shaped you and demonstrate what you learned or how you changed. If you can, pinpoint the transformation and discuss your personal growth.
   5. **Reflect on a time when you questioned or challenged a belief or idea.**
   6. Focus on a time you stood up to others or an experience where your own preconceived view was challenged.
   7. **What is a book you love?**
   8. Your answer should not be a book report. Do not just summarize the plot; instead, detail why you enjoyed this particular text and what it meant to you. What does your favorite book reveal about you? How do you identify with it, and how has it become personal to you?

» The essay should be between 500-700 words.

» Assume you are writing the essay to a person who has no prior knowledge of you. The purpose of the personal statement essay is for the admissions officer to get a glimpse into who you are from your writing, so you must get personal.

- » Be sure that your essay is well-written, error-free, and has excellent grammar.
- » Do *not* follow the rigid five-paragraph essay format of an introduction, three main body paragraphs, followed by a conclusion. Your essay should flow as if you were telling a story to the reader.
- » Read it aloud to get a fresh perspective on how it sounds.
- » When you are done, have others read and provide feedback on your essay. When you return to school, it may be possible to get more input from a language arts teacher or a school counselor.

College Information Resource

Jessica of JLV College Counseling is amazing! (Please forgive me, I just wanted to share that.) To be clear, I do not know her and do not get paid to endorse her work, but I want to promote JLV College Counseling (*jlvcollegecounseling.com*) as a great resource for college information. There is a blog where Jessica provides scholarship opportunities and tips on college searches, college visits, applications, and financial aid. You can also sign up to receive college admissions and scholarship advice. I found her website several years back, and although I have not used this site for college admission advice, her newsletter provided us with reliable scholarship material on a regular basis. Whether it is from this resource or another that you trust, find a reputable way to obtain application tips and scholarship opportunities.

College Scholarship Search

I stated earlier that the leading reasons why students do not apply for scholarships comes down to laziness, busyness, or a lack of organization.

Tenth Grade—Planning for the "Next"

> » Busyness is a direct result of being overwhelmed with the sheer amount of schoolwork, activities, and application requirements during senior year.
> » Lack of organization stems from an unwarranted "I got this" attitude which assumes there is no need to plan because you can deal with things as they come.
> » Laziness usually comes from a lack of ownership, a lack of accountability, or a lack of planning, all of which are rooted in a lack of excellence. Even after finding scholarships to apply for, students often do not have the desire to write the required essays.

I have heard all of the excuses and justifications for why students do not apply for scholarships and witnessed the disappointment that results from insufficient planning. You will not have much time to spare next summer or the start of your senior year, so you should really begin the scholarship process now. Take a moment to look ahead to the suggested timeline for next summer. The sheer volume of tasks will help you understand why building and populating your scholarship document should be your current focus.

Resources such as the JLV website provide many potential scholarship opportunities that may be categorized for your convenience by:

Age	Circumstances
Disability	Gender
Hobbies/Talents	Major
Minority	Parent
Religious	State

Start putting names and links to potential scholarships on your spreadsheet now. The deadlines you record will give you an idea for when they will be due the year you are ready to apply. Some colleges have independent, third-party scholarships listed on their websites designated for only upcoming freshmen to that school. In some cases, you may only be able to see them after you apply, but a search for a college's name plus the word "scholarship" may reveal past recipients that can alert you to their existence. For example, searching for "Auburn University scholarship" reveals that Morgan County Schools in Alabama has a scholarship for incoming freshmen.

Another useful search is for scholarships offered by companies in your area. For example, The Coca-Cola Company offers very nice scholarships each year to local students in Atlanta. Finally, ask around to find local clubs and organizations that give out scholarships. A list of graduating seniors from your area will reveal these types of scholarships that may be an opportunity for you in the future.

Whenever you visit any scholarship website, whether from a college or an independent site, check if they have profiles for previous winners. Seeing the accomplishments of these students can help you better focus on areas you may want to emulate. Another nugget I can share with you is that not all scholarships are limited to seniors. It is very possible to find scholarship opportunities prior to your senior year.

College Tours

During each of my sons' junior year of high school, we used the week of spring break to tour colleges. My youngest son's birthdays usually fell during spring break, so most of them were spent away from home. In the days leading up to spring break of his junior year, he fought me on my requirement of taking a college tour in favor of spending his birthday week at home (he did not win). As we were walking back to the car from the last college stop, he said, "I get it now, Dad. I did not realize that so much went into making a college decision."

Here is our approach to college touring (I call it the "Variety Tour"):

» Research colleges that may potentially be a good fit for you and that you may be interested in attending.

- » Sometime between now (it is not too early!) and midway through next summer, plan a week for visiting colleges (we chose spring break of junior year).
- » Be very particular about the type of colleges you visit. You want to make sure you choose colleges where each of the following categories are represented (recognizing that one college will satisfy multiple categories):
    - › Located in a medium to large city
    - › Located in a small city or rural area
    - › Medium to big school (8,000+ students)
    - › Small to medium school (less than 8,000 students)
        - Include a very small school if that is of interest
    - › Traditional campus with historic buildings and brick walkways
    - › Modern campus
    - › College with the "happiest students" (The Princeton Review)
    - › University with multiple colleges and a wide range of majors
    - › College geared towards a specific discipline (like an engineering school)
- » Try to schedule private appointments in the following areas:
    - › Admissions Office—You may learn of special programs or learn a few admissions tips.
    - › Financial Aid Office—This is an opportunity to learn how to navigate their system and learn of any special scholarship offers firsthand.
    - › College/Department of Your Major—You may be able to get a more in-depth tour, connect with professors, find out about freshman research opportunities, learn about unique or new programs, and possibly learn of departmental scholarships.
    - › Special Programs Office—Many colleges have

school-sponsored programs that support needed areas of growth (e.g. women in STEM, first generation students, Blacks in engineering). These programs usually provide insight not available anywhere else.

College Tour Alternatives:

» Find when college admissions officers may be visiting your area and register to attend those events. These fill up fast! This could look like:
  › Local school visit
  › Small college fair—hosted by a local high school or community center
  › Large college fair—hosted at major event locations and sponsored by groups like National College Fairs (*nacacfairs.org*)
  › Information sessions in your area—hosted by organizations like *ExploringEducationalExcellence.org*

When scheduled early enough, the first college tour is for learning about the many aspects of college life. Visiting all the different styles of colleges above will give you a much better idea of the campus environment you want for four years. Knowing the style of college you prefer will help to narrow down options while you build your initial pool of potential colleges. Come decision time, having this perspective will be much appreciated.

As you go on these tours, be sure to document as much as you can about each school so that you will be able to recall the pros and cons.

> **Parents**: I took it upon myself to do the documentation, which allowed my boys to enjoy the experience. Immediately after the tour, I would ask what they thought about different aspects of the visit so I could document their personal thoughts.

We were also intentional about talking to random students during our college visits, and we encourage you to do the same. This will help you get a feel for the friendliness of the campus and you will likely receive some good, honest feedback that is not coming from your guide who is being paid to tell you all the nice things about the school.

At a minimum, you want to listen to the information session and take the campus tour. The best visits were the ones we personalized ourselves as we learned things that are not shared in the info session. We also did everything possible to find a contact at the school that could arrange a personal tour even if we took the official tour. Here are a few of the benefits from our personal tours:

- » Before attending a tour with my middle son, a friend of ours arranged a personal introduction with the head of admissions. After meeting with Brian, he strongly suggested that my son apply for their elite scholarships; this is the very scholarship that has taken him to study abroad at Oxford and visit Indonesia.
- » On a prearranged personal tour, Aaron and I met with six students in his intended major and met with the dean of the college. We also met with a financial aid officer and learned about a new all-expenses paid scholarship that was not yet listed on the school's main scholarship website (he received an equivalent scholarship to this school).
- » At another university, a student we knew insisted we visit the director of a support program specially designated for Aaron's major. After meeting with the director, she set up an impromptu Q&A and then recommended him for a departmental scholarship that he was eventually offered.
- » During another personal tour, Aaron and I inadvertently met the wife of the dean for the Honors College, who scheduled a personal meeting for us. After meeting the dean, he recommended my son apply for their elite scholarship—the very scholarship he is on now.

I know these may be unique stories, but each of these encounters led to scholarships opportunities for my boys; therefore, I believe this is worth the effort. Did this always work for us? No. One of our top choice schools where we experienced that personal touch twice did not offer either of my kids a scholarship, which was a bit surprising to me.

Summer Programs or Activities—Additional Ideas

You must take advantage of the summers prior to your junior and senior years in order to build your application content. The more you can demonstrate unique passion (strong interest) or leadership, the more impactful your "WOW" factor will be for college acceptance and scholarships.

My two younger sons, Brian and Aaron realized that the high school students in their community faced a shortcoming in college preparation. They spent a summer creating a nonprofit organization to address this issue, built a website to host the program, recruited adult volunteers to assist, worked with school officials to implement their solution, then started the program that fall as school began. Both of them were able to use this experience on their college applications, and it was a major talking point at their college interviews.

While in high school, Brian's choice for a college major was computer science. During the summer after his sophomore year, he was only able to secure a single one-week program in addition to a Christian summer camp. Together, we decided to register him in an online computer science class to learn Java. Not only did this give him coding experience before going to college, it also demonstrated to admissions officers his determination to learn within his chosen field given that his high school did not offer sufficient classes.

Ideally, at least part of this summer is already planned, and you have a summer program(s) and/or job lined up. If not, this list of alternative summer activities still has great options:

- » READ!!! Find a couple of fun books to read over the summer. Many colleges ask, "What is one of your favorite books and why?" You can visit my website at *woolfolkworks.com/readinglist* for book recommendations.
- » Plan to create a new club at your school. This type of endeavor can be fun, especially when done with a friend or two.
- » Develop a plan to address a problem in your school or community.
- » Research online or virtual classes that may still be available.
- » Use online resources to learn a new skill.
- » Do volunteer work.
- » Create your own work opportunity (such as mowing lawns or babysitting).
- » Commit to a physical workout plan.

Discipline—Consistency

"Success isn't always about greatness. It's about consistency. Consistent hard work leads to success. Greatness will come."
–Dwayne "The Rock" Johnson

The fifth and final "Element of Discipline" to be addressed is consistency, which is an offshoot of excellence. I am sure you have heard the fable of the tortoise and the hare. I am not advocating for the slowness of the tortoise but against the haphazard attitude of the hare, because the steady truly does win the race. No matter your capability, your consistency will be a strong determinant of your measured ability. **The smartest person in a classroom will not always end up with the highest grade; a smart person with consistency usually does**. Understanding why everything you do matters will help to deal with your "I don't feel like it" moments, and a mindset of excellence will encourage you to do the best you can under whatever circumstances

Before The Application

you are facing. *You cannot always control the situation or circumstances in which you find yourself, but you can always control your reactions to them.* Discipline is a mindset that you choose to have every day.

High School Resumé

This summer, build the first draft of your high school resumé that can be updated as time goes on. This is another task you should do now while you have the time. When you actually need your official resumé, you will be *so* happy that it is already designed and contains all of your basic information. All you will have to do is update and send it. When it comes to the style of resumé to build, you will never be able to satisfy all the critics. Whatever style you choose, make sure it is polished, complete, and accurate. Only include items that have value to the reader. Before you add anything, ask yourself, "Why would the reader care?" Prioritize the resumé in an order that highlights your most important attributes first. Most people are lazy readers and may only spend 15-20 seconds looking at it on the first pass.

Social Media Footprint

> *"Congress shall make no law ... or abridging the freedom of speech..."*
> *—First Amendment*

Freedom of speech is defined as the right to express any opinions without governmental censorship or restraint. Our constitution gives us the right to free speech (albeit with a few exceptions). However, please understand that your legal right does **not** mean you can freely say whatever you want and does **not** absolve you from the consequences of your words or actions; this is especially true on social media. People are denied jobs, unable to secure loans, and destroying relationships because of inappropriate posts. You have a personal brand that you build over four years of high school and beyond. All your hard work can be put at risk by one offensive comment on social media.

Carefully review all your social media accounts that may portray an image of you that could work against your college application profile. This applies to posts, comments, and pictures associated with your online profile. Colleges do not want their name associated with negative publicity. Do not think that privacy settings or alternate names will guarantee protection. You should review *everything* going back at least to the start of high school and be conscious of things you put online going forward.

Eleventh Grade—Putting a Stamp on Your Brand

You must build the identity you
will promote to colleges!

"You can't build a reputation on what you are going to do."
—Henry Ford

Note: If this is the first chapter that you are reading in this book, I highly recommend that you go back and read the preceding chapters before continuing. You will find valuable information for application prep and college readiness. Also, some information presented in this chapter is dependent on material covered in previous parts of the book.

No matter where you currently stand in your effort to build your ideal college profile, you are still in a position to positively impact your standing in the college admissions process next year. If you need to go back and apply some of the principles previously shared in this book, do so. If you are on track, then keep pushing forward. Never give up on yourself and never stop striving to grow.

In this chapter, I am providing a model for the junior year wheel needed to "drive off" towards college success. Our objective is to:

» Continue to grasp the value of **reading regularly** and **ACT/SAT prep**

Before The Application

- » Understand the difference between a **performer** and a **learner**
- » Learn the value of **study groups**
- » **Develop your passion or strong interest**
- » Appreciate the value of **building relationships**
- » Realize the benefit of using **social media** to promote your brand
  - › Perform action items towards building your ideal college admissions profile:
  - › Increase your activity involvement
  - › Seek out any help you need
  - › Expand your research and build your list of colleges of interest
  - › Research programs and activities for the upcoming summer
  - › Participate in college tours
  - › Review your transcript for accuracy
  - › Ramp up your ACT/SAT prep
  - › Ensure you have a productive summer
  - › **Educate yourself on the dynamics of the college application process**

Junior Focus Point: McDonald's, Apple, Rolex, Coca-Cola, Dell, Ford, Kellogg's, Microsoft. Are there any Americans who do not know what each of these brands represent? Imagine you are invited to a dinner to celebrate a major accomplishment. You are told to dress your best and expect to have the fanciest meal of your life. What would your reaction be if your limo pulled into the parking lot of a McDonald's? Your destination would not meet your expectation because the McDonald's brand is not about fancy dining but quality fast food. Now imagine how excited you would be if your next birthday present came in a box that has "Rolex" on the side. Before you even open it, your excitement level would begin to skyrocket. Even though most of us have never owned a Rolex, we associate the highest level of quality and prestige with that brand. We form this association through advertisements and representations in media that inform us of the quality that comes with a particular name brand.

All successful companies have to first identify the market that they have the resources to reach and make a quality product that will appeal to those consumers. Then they must advertise in order to inform customers about the existence and quality of their product. In order for you to become the student equivalent of a Rolex, a Mercedes-Benz, an iPhone, or a pair of Air Jordans, you must first identify the tier of school you are targeting and work to become a high-quality applicant. Then you must advertise your personal brand so that you are recognized as the desired quality of student by your dream schools. The true purpose of this book is to teach you how to place yourself in a position that clearly demonstrates the value you will bring to your target university. Your junior year is when you put a stamp on your brand. You only have one more year to build your college profile before it is application season; let's make sure that you use it wisely.

The Fundamentals— Solidifying the Core

The key components, as expected, are Reading and ACT/SAT Prep.

Reading for Fun

If you are reading regularly, keep up the good work! However, I know that some of you are still doing everything possible to avoid reading just like I did at your age. We have to recognize that there are consequences to all of our actions. I pray your plan is not to go through life running away from the things you do not like or are not good at. Avoidance will stop you from growing as a student, as a valuable member of society, and even as a person. Choosing to not read frequently is a disadvantage in the classroom, on tests, and in life. Most of us who do not care to

Before The Application

read have other less effective practices that we believe will carry us through, such as relying on friends to help us or using study-guides like CliffsNotes. But just like all shortcuts, they can only carry us so far.

Emma Watson and Oprah Winfrey are probably the most well-known avid readers in America, but they are not alone. Did you know that Mindy Kaling named her character on *The Mindy Project* after one of her favorite authors, Jhumpa Lahiri? Or that Lebron James uses books as his means to focus before games and has Suzanne Collins's *Hunger Games* trilogy on his reading list? Or that one of Bill Gates' favorite books of the last decade is Steven Pinker's *Better Angels of our Nature*, which takes a long and profound look at the reduction of violence and discrimination over time.

Reading Check-In!

Did you complete your reading challenge?

  I was able to finish _____ books over the last year

 The **Commitment to Reading Challenge** will continue over the next year. Pick the option that best fits how you wish to track your reading. For example, challenge yourself to read one book per month or for at least two hours per week.

  I *will* read a minimum of _____ books over the next year.

–OR–

I *will* read a minimum of _____ hours per week over the next year.

 For suggestions on reading material, you can still refer to the Helen Ruffin Reading Bowl Booklist and Project Lit. You can also visit my website at *woolfolkworks.com/readinglist* for my sons' Top 10 Reading List and book recommendations shared by readers of this book just like you. In addition to reading for fun, you should begin to read articles that will help you keep up with current events. Colleges may ask questions to gauge your awareness of the things that shape the world you live in.

ACT/SAT Prep

If you have been committed to excellence in the classroom and have been doing the proper ACT/SAT prep work for the past two years, you are well on your way to obtaining your optimal score on your choice of college entrance exams. If you have not been putting in the work or if you have not progressed towards your optimal score, you have time to catch up or fine tune your test skills. Do not stop utilizing your Test Question of the Day app until you have taken your final test. You should also continue doing one timed section of the test about every other weekend or so.

I am often asked which test a student should take, and my answer is **both**! The two tests are very similar but also have significant differences that may make one more suited for you. Here are the 11 key differences as noted by PrepScholar:

1. **Time Per Question**—The SAT gives you more time per question than the ACT.
2. **Science Section**—The ACT contains a section entirely devoted to science, the SAT does not.
3. (The SAT *does* test scientific concepts—just not through a separate Science section.)
4. **No Calculator Math Subsection**—The SAT contains a "no calculator" math subsection for which you may not use a calculator.
5. **Types and Balance of Math Concepts**—The ACT has a much

larger focus on geometry and tests a few concepts that the SAT does not test at all (such as matrices, graphs of trig functions, and logarithms).

6. **Math Formulas Reference Guide**—The SAT provides you with a diagram of math formulas, whereas the ACT does not.
7. **Importance of Math in Final Score**—On the ACT, math accounts for ***one-fourth*** of your total score, whereas on the SAT, math accounts for ***half*** of your total score.
8. **Number of Answer Choices on Math**—While ACT math gives you five possible answer choices, SAT math only gives you four.
9. **Grid-In Math Questions**—The SAT has grid-ins, which are questions for which you must fill in your own answer, ACT math only has multiple-choice questions.
10. **Evidence-Support Reading Questions**—Evidence-support questions are a big part of SAT Reading but are entirely absent from ACT Reading.
11. **Chronological Reading Questions**—On SAT reading, all questions given to you follow a chronological order, but on ACT reading, questions can flow randomly.
12. **Essay Content**—On the SAT, your essay will dissect the author's argument using evidence and reasoning. On the ACT writing section, you will also give your own opinion on the issue.

Our strategy was to take both the ACT and SAT in the fall of junior year, about a month apart in October and November. The purpose of this timing was to determine which test each one was best suited for and how much more prep work we needed to put in, if any.

» During his junior year, Christopher only took the SAT, not the ACT. With him being my oldest, a lot of the philosophies discussed in this book were not in place yet. We realized his performance was well short of what we considered to be his optimal score. Over the next year, he hunkered down to make the necessary strategy improvements, and his score as a senior improved by over 200 points. We then had him take the ACT with no preparation specific to the test, and he obtained a noticeably better score as compared to the SAT. Even without dedicated preparation, his scores proved that he was better suited for taking the ACT. This is how I learned the lesson to consider which test is best for a student to prepare for.

» Thankfully, we had a four-year gap between the first two sons to adjust our plan of action. Brian took the SAT his junior year and MISSION ACCOMPLISHED—optimal score achieved. Before getting the score back, he took the ACT as scheduled. The result again was MISSION ACCOMPLISHED! In the fall of his junior year, he was done taking college entrance exams. We were able to cross this milestone off his college prep list and concentrate on other areas.

» Two years later, it was time for Aaron to take both tests in the fall of his junior year. His results on the SAT were *so* close to his optimal score that we considered not taking it again. After some discussion, *he* made the decision to press on and work towards surpassing this result. Once we received his ACT score and saw that it was well under his optimal score, we simply ignored it and chose to focus solely on the SAT. A year later, he blew past what we originally thought was his optimal score.

I shared these stories to stress that you must determine the best test for you, that there is no perfect timeline for when you will get your optimal score, and that proper preparation will yield favorable results. Taking the ACT and/or SAT during your junior year can be less stressful if you treat them as just another part of your preparation for when the test truly matters during senior year. However, lower stress may actually help to produce surprisingly good scores and build confidence.

Special Note: I used the term "optimal score" quite a few times, so you may be asking yourself how you can determine yours. While there is no exact formula for calculating an optimal score, I do want to clarify my usage of the term:

» Your optimal score is a projected ceiling based on an honest assessment of yourself as a student. It should be estimated based on an evaluation of your knowledge, ability, test taking skills, drive, determination, commitment, reading comprehension skills, analytical skills, confidence level, etc. Your optimal score is not based on the best you could do if everything went perfectly nor is it based on the score needed to get into a specific college.

» A target score is determined by looking at the middle 50% range of the previous year's incoming freshman class for a desired college.

For some students, a target score for a dream school on their list dictates what they choose as their optimal score. In our household, my sons strived for their optimal score and allowed their actual score to dictate which schools would be added to their college list.

ACT/SAT Score Tracker

It is time to record any new scores from over the past year and track the progress you have made. Doing so will let you know if you are on the right track or if you need to improve your prep strategy. Remember that if testing independently, you can *estimate* your score by using the Raw Score Conversion Table on the College Board's website or the Sample ACT Scoring Chart on The Princeton Review's website.

Junior Essentials—Taking Responsibility

Transition from Performer to Learner

Many college-bound high school students mainly focus on end metrics. For them, success in the classroom is measured by grades, scores, GPA, etc. Students that are primarily driven by these metrics have often mastered the art of achieving great results without necessarily mastering the content. Prioritizing memorization over learning in order to obtain shortsighted goals is what it means to be a "performer" in education. But let me be fair—these goals are forced upon students by the system. High schools have created an environment where high metric achievers are celebrated, and colleges highlight the very same metrics for their incoming class of freshmen. Often, the top students at a school are even referred to as "high *performers*" or "top *performers*"!

These metrics should not be the primary goal of education; instead, the results of properly succeeding in learning should be the true goal of school. In order to become a college-ready student, your junior year should be about transforming from being performance-focused to learning-focused. Failing to adopt this skillset now will result in you not learning the material being taught in your college prep courses. This will cost you once you enter college because you will be missing the proper foundation needed for classes at the next level.

While sitting in a session during a college orientation, we heard an excellent speaker explain to the students that focusing mainly on getting good grades—just as they did in high school—will be their downfall at the college level. He explained that in college you must be focused on learning and not just performing, reinforcing the same words I shared with my children throughout their lives. In order not to struggle to make this transition during your freshman year of college, I urge you to start this adjustment now, while still in high school.

Before The Application

My sons did not have to make this transition while in high school because this was a mindset instilled in them throughout their years of education. A couple of things I taught them from a young age may help you in making your own transition:

› The first concept is simply asking the question, "Why?" The principle of asking "why" is found in the "Five Whys" (sometimes referred to as "5Y") technique, which is used to quickly get to the root of a problem by using deductive reasoning. The basic premise is to ask the question "Why?" about anything you learn, and then based on the answer, ask the question "Why?" again. Repeating this process leads to a deeper understanding of any concept.

› My wife, Dr. Dedra Woolfolk, is Dean of the College of Arts and Sciences at Point University and has taught biology there for over fifteen years. I randomly asked her to give me one of the basic concepts taught in her class, and then I asked the five whys.

The Concept: In the process of cellular respiration, the energy released from breaking down the food we eat is used to make ATP.

1. **Why do we need ATP?** ATP provides the energy for our cells to perform many essential chemical reactions.
2. **Why is this important?** The essential chemical reactions are necessary for vital cellular processes to take place.
3. **Why is this important?** If vital cellular processes cease, cells will eventually die.
4. **Why does this matter?** If cells die, tissues die.
5. **Why does this matter?** If tissues die, organs and organ systems fail, leading to death.

I now understand that the food we eat keeps us alive through cellular respiration. When I hear that food gives us energy, I know that refers to ATP. Without ATP, our cells die. The 5Y method can be applied to any field or subject to gain a deeper understanding!

» I call the next concept "The Student Becomes the Teacher." If you want to confirm that you have actually learned something, go explain it to someone else. The concept is similar to the quote attributed to Albert Einstein, "If you can't explain it to a six-year-old, you don't understand it yourself." This also doubles as a great study tip. Even if you must talk to yourself in the mirror, explaining a concept out loud will let you know if you have moved past the level of just understanding. I use this trick whenever I get stuck on a problem. Before asking for help, I first try talking through the problem out loud. I often come to the answer before the person who is helping me ever says a word.

» The final concept is "The World is Your Classroom." Education should not be limited to the curriculum taught in a school building. When you come across items of interest, pursue a greater knowledge of the subject matter through exploration. Additionally, there are many things about life that are not taught in the classroom that you should prepare for as you build towards your independence.

Understand that primarily focusing on learning does not contradict the emphasis I placed on the importance of your GPA. With respect to getting into college, metrics still matter, so having your best possible GPA is important. The good news is that having a predominant focus on learning does not mean your grades must suffer, as I have been preparing you for this moment. When you combine the three tenets of (1) always putting forth your best effort, (2) incorporating the elements of discipline, and (3) the prioritization of learning, I believe you will end up with your desired grades AND be well positioned for learning at the college level.

My sons combined the three tenets above to achieve many great academic accomplishments, including my youngest being valedictorian in a class of 540+ students. Even if they had chosen to be performers for the sake of a great GPA, class rank was still out of their control. My youngest two sons had nearly identical GPAs, yet Brian was ranked number seven in his class and Aaron was number one. My sons' rankings were not what was most important, but the combination of their effort towards excellence, their learning class content, and their college application profile was. They both were accepted to the same levels of school and are each attending college on scholarships that are among the top in the country. Equally as important, they were both prepared to be successful on the college level.

Another benefit of focusing on being a learner is that you can progress through school without stressing over being the top performer in your class. In 2017, two young men from the same public high school had very similar SAT scores and college application profiles. One was valedictorian, and the other's GPA was about 7 points behind (on a 100-point scale). Today, both are attending Harvard University, which goes to show that when you have a strong overall college profile, a very good GPA will serve you just as well as a great GPA.

The purpose of making the transition from "performer" to "learner" is to become a student that approaches education as an opportunity to learn, not just to pass a class or get an A. Education should be an essential part of your plan to achieve many of your life's goals, not just a check mark for getting into college. I do recognize that there will be times when you must think like a performer in order to generate your best GPA, and this is okay. The transition to being primarily a learner means the need to perform will be the exception and not the norm.

Study Groups

Continuing the theme of being college ready, I want to highlight the value of study groups while in high school and college. Participating in study groups prior to junior year is fine, but I waited to recommend it until this stage because study groups can potentially do more harm than good without the right maturity level. The most important factor is to find like-minded classmates that are as serious about school as you are. You can choose to work with one group of students that share the same coursework as you or have a separate group for each class. The ideal size for a study group is four to five students. Here are some tips for a good study group:

- » **Ask each other the question "Why?"**—Use the 5Y technique to help one another become better learners.
- » **Alternate being the teacher**—Each member should have the chance to teach the material to the rest of the group.
- » **Find the missing piece**—It is nearly impossible for one person to capture all the information presented in a class and have a complete understanding of all requirements for an assignment or upcoming exam. Having a group helps fill in the gaps for items you may not even realize you were missing.
- » **Hold each other accountable**—Not allowing your friends to give up or do subpar work helps them to remember that *everything you/they do matters.*
- » **Motivate one another**—Positive peer pressure will push you to uphold your *mindset of excellence.*
- » **Stay organized and focused**—Have a group leader for every study session (this role can rotate) because it is important to stay on task and not allow anyone to dominate a session.

It is not easy for everyone to participate in study groups (especially true introverts) and some students simply prefer to study alone. Even so, I am a true believer that the benefits clearly make this effort worth it. Study groups also provide readily available resources if you ever have to miss class for any reason. Finally, remember that iron sharpens iron, so use the peers in your study group to help you grow.

Before The Application

Develop Your Passion or Strong Interest

Demonstrated passion or strong interest should be an important piece of your college application resumé. A passion is something you truly care so much about that you feel as if you have no choice but to act. You can demonstrate your passion by:

- » Committing to the development of a skillset (sports, the arts, academics, etc.)
- » Creating and implementing a solution to some problem (such as addressing a school or community concern)
- » Taking actions towards making an impact (such as standing up for human rights)

Your demonstrated passion can be diving into an academic skill set or taking an extracurricular activity to a national level or becoming nationally ranked in a sport or creating a non-profit to help your community or starting a business from an idea you created or _____ (you fill in the blank!). Colleges care about demonstrated passion because of the level of commitment it takes to excel at a very high level.

Developing a strong interest in an area that captures your attention can also demonstrate a substantial level of commitment, albeit to a lesser extent than a passion. My youngest son Aaron attended many summer math programs throughout high school, and his older brother Brian attended many summer debate programs. Aaron was president of the math club and attended the four-week Governor's Honors Program in math, while Brian competed in a national debate competition at the University of Southern California. Aaron organized the first math competition at his high school. Brian helped to organize the first debate tournament.

On the surface, it may seem that they both had similar accomplishments in their respective fields. However, through his applications, essays, and interviews, Aaron was able to reveal a deep passion for his interest that Brian admittedly lacked. Aaron served as a volunteer math tutor, created the math club, fought for a sponsor, secured funding, and attended math competitions alone so he could gain information to train his peers. He dedicated countless hours to researching and developing a theory to disprove the definition of "division by zero" as being undefined in his free time. Brian portrayed a strong interest by demonstrating his high level of commitment to debate, *which definitely looked good on a college application*, but Aaron's intense devotion raised his profile to another level.

Having interests and not driving any of them to the level of a strong interests or a demonstrated passion sends another message to colleges: a lack of commitment. Consider why colleges care to offer students academic scholarships. One reason is the ability to boast about the quality of students they are able to attract. Another reason is that colleges will gain walking advertisements as their alumni go out and make their mark on the world. This is why students whose passions lead to them making a major difference are often recruited and offered the best scholarships.

Building Relationships

Most college applications will require letters of recommendation from at least two teachers and your school counselor. This is an important part of your college application packet, so every effort should be made to ensure that your letters will stand out. Counselors rarely see many of their students until they are seniors coming to them with requests about college applications. Teachers have told me that they regret having to write letters of recommendation, because they struggle to come up with something to say for most students. All three of my boys had glowing letters of recommendation from their counselors and their teachers because our family had a genuine relationship with each of them.

It is time to learn that life is all about relationships. You never actually deal with businesses, the government, or colleges. You always deal with the *individuals* who represent these entities. This is why I stress the importance of building relationships with people. I do not encourage you to be insincere, but to establish genuine relationships with people that may have influence in your life. Many of your letters of recommendation are likely to come from your eleventh-grade teachers which is why you should focus on relationships at this stage.

Make it a point to have real conversations with your teachers. Ask them how they are doing and ask about their lives, such as where they are from, where they went to school, or how long they have been teaching. Go to their tutorial sessions even if you only need a little extra help or want to discuss a topic beyond what was taught in the classroom. Talk to them about the industry or any interests related to the subject they teach. Ask for their opinion on options you are considering like college majors or careers. Find out if they know of any academic programs outside of school that they feel you may be a good fit for. If you let them get to know you, they will be more than willing to write a recommendation letter for you, and it will be much easier for them to do so.

Realistically speaking, you may not be able to make a connection with all your teachers, so consider carefully which relationships you will build. Try to establish a relationship with a teacher closely associated with your intended college major field and with teachers that you naturally connect with. There is always the chance that your future college major will change or that a teacher will leave the school before they can write you a recommendation. This will not prevent you from receiving a very good recommendation, especially if you follow the tips I will provide during your senior year. Having positive relationships greatly increases your chances for glowing recommendations.

With respect to your counselor, I suggest that you stop by at least once every month or so for a brief conversation. Give them a quick update on your activities and accomplishments. Your high school professional counselor can stand between you and a college acceptance or scholarship. In addition to supplying colleges with important facts and an evaluation of your course load, a counselor may have the option to provide a recommendation. Regular interactions with your counselor will help them speak highly of you in this situation. Many colleges expect to see a recommendation from a counselor, and some may interpret the absence of one as a negative against you. Competitive colleges (<50% acceptance rate) are even known to call counselors to assist with decisions on final spots.

A counselor may be reluctant to speak up for you if your history with them has not been pleasant. If they do wish to be a champion for you, they will either write a subpar recommendation or refrain from writing one at all. Establishing a positive relationship with your counselor before your senior year improves your chances of receiving a high-praising recommendation.

Special Note: *If you give your teachers a gift for Christmas and/or Teacher Appreciation Day, include your counselor!*

> **Parents**: It very much helped that I was an active parent at my kids' school. I was on the School Governance Council and President of the Parent Booster Club for our school's magnet program. The teachers, counselors, and principal regularly saw me at the school advocating for all students and showing appreciation to all teachers. Counselors and teachers told me directly that they went out of their way to support my kids because I went out of my way to support the school.

Social Media Branding

The question of how often admissions officers review prospective students' social media profiles is unknown. Yet, the possibility of it happening is real, which presents you with an opportunity. I have already discussed how social media can negatively affect you, so now the question is how you can use it to your advantage.

Here are a few ways you can make use of your social media pages:

» Do not make your pages private
» Highlight your awards and recognitions and thank those that helped you achieve them
» Post educational materials and ways for others to get involved in the volunteer activities you care about
» Tag yourself in articles that portray excellence you achieved in an activity
» Upload videos that showcase your skills and talents

Junior Timeline—Remain Steadfast

START OF SCHOOL

Julia Says

At this point, I hope that you are building on what you have discovered about yourself, because this is when you are going to need it most. Junior year is the last year you will have to bulk up your college resume. Plus, your junior year transcript is the first thing colleges see when reading your application. With this in mind, I highly recommend prioritizing your passions and your schoolwork. This is when you are going to have to use everything you gained from your efforts towards self-discovery thus far and put it all together. Even if you have not figured everything out, there is still a great strategy for maintaining your mental health and your schoolwork. The key is your environment.

Your environment is essentially what makes you, you. It is the place that dictates how you act, what you learn, and even your identity. Exploring different environments is a great way to discover yourself for your mental wellness, while also helping with your productivity. Since your environment is such a big part of your life, it is up to you to discover what environment works best for you and your work regiment. For example, I love being outside. When I am outside, it makes all of my work less stressful, because I am being productive in the environment that is best suited for me. You should find something similar. You have to discover what environment will reduce your stress so that you can work for longer without pushing your limits too far. You can create your own space or even move around if you are a bit more nomadic. Finding the right environment is key to being productive with little to no cost to your mental wellness.

Expand Activity Involvement

In about a year, you will be filling out the Activities and Leadership sections of your college applications, and ideally, you have been building up to this over the past couple of years. Write down a list that includes up to five activities, programs, or clubs you have participated in. For each item, you should be able to do more than state the title you held and give a description of the activity or organization. You should be able to describe the tangible results of your individual contributions. Or you should be able to take it to the next level and describe how your leadership and initiative were able to make a direct impact that would have been impossible without your involvement. If you have been properly updating your Activity Log, this task should be pretty straightforward. Either way, this is your heads-up that you have one year to create descriptions for each of your activities.

By now you should be a part of at least one group, club, or organization that can provide you with the opportunity for a major leadership role. If you are not positioned for a major role, seek a minor role now and then shoot for a major role for your senior year. If you have already had a minor role, do not shy away from pursuing a major role. If you are not able to secure an official role, do not allow the absence of a title hinder you from participating and demonstrating leadership.

Before The Application

Special Note: You may want to explore other areas beyond your known interests, and joining a club or organization is a great way to expose yourself to new potential career pursuits. This may also present novel opportunities to give back to your community.

Finally, now is a good time to review your Activity Log to make sure all activities are properly documented. Keep it up to date so that you can pull from it during application season.

THANKSGIVING BREAK

Evaluation Time

Around this time freshman year, I suggested that you assess your first few months of the semester to ensure you were getting a strong start to your high school career. I recommend a similar evaluation period this Thanksgiving break. Typically, junior year is when the bulk of your college prep level courses begin, and I hope you have put yourself in a position that challenges you academically. Do your best to not fall behind as you get accustomed to a higher level of thinking.

As your courses get tougher, finding quality help also gets harder. Be sure to explore all available resources at your disposal. Here are a few suggestions for getting extra help:

» **Teacher after-school hours**—Extra time with your teacher may be beneficial. However, sometimes a teacher simply does not fit your learning style. If you cannot switch classes, talk with a teacher who teaches the same class and ask to attend their after-school sessions.
» **Study groups**—If you have not done so already, start or join a study group. You may find that your peers are your best teachers.
» **Online resources**—There are so many online resources available to you today. When our school was without a physics teacher

for an extended period of time, Brian made his way through physics using Khan Academy and YouTube.
- » **Effective tutoring**—If your family decides to hire a tutor, be sure to screen for one that has a reputation for effective tutoring.

A lot of money can be wasted on ineffective tutoring. If you need a tutor, you want to make sure you get the help that you truly need. There are many educators who are great teachers, but their skill set does not necessarily translate well to tutoring. Personally, I am not the greatest teacher but an excellent tutor. The difference is in the approach.

- » *Teachers present the material.* Good teachers present the material so that most students comprehend it. Great teachers do all that and motivate their students to want to learn.
- » *Tutors should not start with the material but with the student.* Good tutors will assess the student's knowledge, find the gaps, and fill them in. Great tutors will understand how a student thinks and teach them how to learn the material using their learning style; then they will make sure the student understands the "whys" behind the information so they can figure it out for themselves the next time.

In summary, a teacher's job is to spend more time talking, while a tutor's role is to spend most of the time asking questions and listening.

Research Colleges of Interest

Whether you have a good idea regarding your future college major or not, you hopefully have an idea for a field of study. During this break, do some research into colleges that are well known for your potential major(s) or at least have strong programs in your general area of interest. If you are not yet at the point where you have even decided on a general area of study, be sure that you are researching colleges that have a wide variety of majors. This will allow you to select a future major from a college with a good overall reputation. There is an assortment of websites that offer rankings of colleges not only by overall categories, but also based on specific disciplines. You can also do a search for the best colleges for specific majors or intended careers. This is a great way to start building your pool of potential colleges so that you can do more in-depth research on each of them. Your goal is to build a list of at least five colleges you like.

Start filling in your College Tracking Spreadsheet for colleges that are high on your list and consider adding them to your college tour list. Use any available resources to connect with current students, former students, and/or staff at colleges of interest. It is very possible that by calling the admissions office, you can be put in touch with student representatives who will be glad to speak with you. Reach out to your "**network,**" which in this case is your family, friends, classmates, professional school counselor, teachers, community organizations, etc.

It is okay to fall in love with a single college, but DO NOT allow this to blind you to another college that may actually be a better fit. I do not believe that there is only one ideal college for each student. Many factors go into the final decision for where you will attend college, but you should not make that decision until you have all the data, the most important of which is the financial package.

Prior to spring of his senior year, Brian was adamant that he would not attend an in-state college. He had no plans to even apply to one, but I insisted so that he would have a "safe school" on his list (in this case "safe" meant one that he knew he could afford). Days before the college decision deadline, he was still determined to attend the University of Southern California, where he was accepted into the Honors program for their College of Engineering on a half-tuition scholarship. But ultimately, the amazing scholarship he received from the University of Georgia just made the most sense, so he resigned to stay in-state. Today, he cannot imagine being anywhere else!

CHRISTMAS BREAK

Research Summer Programs

I have already established that this break is the ideal time to research summer programs in areas like leadership, academic research, arts, STEM (robotics, coding, game design), social issues, music, etc. For every program you will consider applying to, document the start/end date, the date the application opens, application deadlines, any requirements to complete the application, the cost, and the description. For free and low-cost programs, you want to apply within a few days of the application opening for your best chance to secure a spot. If available to you, take advantage of overnight programs because of the added benefit they provide in preparation for "leaving the nest."

The summer before your senior year is a good time to participate in programs that show your commitment to an area of study you may be considering for a college major. Internships and volunteer work are great routes to accomplish this goal, as well as shadowing a professional for a few days. These options can provide a lot of experience with little cost. Get creative in your research and make the most of this upcoming summer!

Colleges of Interest

Before applying to any schools, you must first build a college interest pool. This is a list of all colleges you may be interested in attending for any variety of reasons. Your pool should include schools that are strong in your major, where you satisfy the requirements for their competitive scholarship(s), or that meet any other criteria you may have. Also look for local colleges that may offer the best fit for a college budget. Make your pool as large as you like but keep it within reason because you will only be making it harder for yourself when you have to narrow down your list.

Before The Application

As you add colleges to your interest pool, list at least one reason why they are being added. You should use this list to populate your College Tracking Spreadsheet with only the schools that you are truly interested in applying to. This is not a one-time exercise. Continue to populate the interest pool as you learn more over the next year.

College interest goes both ways. When asked, most colleges say that "demonstrated interest" does not influence their decision, but I believe that this is a gray area. Colleges *do* track and give weight to the interactions you have with them. If they take the time to do all of that, then they obviously care about you demonstrating your interest to some extent. Colleges likely deny this because they do not want to go back to the time when students inundated admissions offices with frivolous contact in hopes of standing out. When it comes down to deciding between candidates, admissions officers would rather offer acceptance to someone they believe is seriously considering their school as an option. You can demonstrate your interest by visiting the college in person (official visit), taking virtual tours, visiting their booth at a local college fair, and selecting their college through an application portal or a college-matching website. You should sign up to receive emails and join their mailing list. They can track your activity on their emails, so when you receive one from them, open it and click on any links that interest you.

When you register for the ACT or SAT, there is a set of optional questions about your course load, extracurricular activities and accomplishments, college interests, etc. Use the answers to your advantage because your responses, along with your test score, may put you on their recruitment radar. If the college has a particularly strong interest in you and you show an interest in them, they may even offer perks like a paid visit to campus or a suggestion of scholarships to apply for. Another benefit of completing the detailed profile is that you can use the information colleges will send you to find potential schools for your college interest pool.

SAT Subject Tests™

As of January of 2021, the College Board organization no longer offers SAT Subject Tests™ in the U.S. These tests were designed to assess your knowledge of a variety of subjects at the high school level, and normally this would be the ideal time to begin your preparation for these exams. This decision was intended to reduce demands on students applying to college.

SPRING BREAK

College Tours

College tours fill up quickly during high school spring breaks, so be sure to reserve your time early. If you have not done a "Variety Tour" yet (see the Summer Break section of sophomore year), I recommend that you do that now. If you have already completed that version of a tour, use this time to visit colleges in which you have a strong interest.

If possible, arrange for a personalized tour of the schools you like. Reach out to the admissions office, financial aid office, and the honors college (if appropriate) for appointments. Reach out to your "network" to try to find someone who has a connection to staff or students associated with the college to help with your personalized tour. At one university we visited, we knew two students who had different majors than what my son was interested in, yet they arranged for us to meet up with six students in his desired major. They took us on a tour of the entire campus, paying extra attention to the college that housed his intended major. Going out to lunch with these students gave us a great opportunity to ask personal questions regarding their experiences at the school.

While on a personalized tour, you want to gather information about things they may not share on a standard tour, such as:

» Does the college offer a computer repair service?

Before The Application

- » Does the school have a policy for missing class due to illness or does this vary by professor?
- » Does the school provide helpful and individualized guidance to students for building their class schedule?
- » How difficult is it to find parking?
- » How easy or difficult is it to get your required classes at registration time?
- » How is the food?
- » Which dining halls are open during nights and weekends and what hours are they open?
- » Is the student culture more collaborative or competitive?
- » What are the security concerns regarding safety and theft?
- » What health services are offered by the college and what are their hours of operation?
- » What is the grading system? Is it a universal policy or does it vary by professor?
- » What quality off-campus housing options are in walking distance?

Also consider any questions that may be of specific importance to you, such as:

- » Are there any concerns regarding diversity on campus?
- » Does security offer rides around campus during late hours?
- » How does the ticket policy work for sporting events?

Special Note: You may want to take pictures while on your visit and post them on your social media while being sure to tag the school.

Summer Programs or Activities

Follow up and confirm that everything is in order on any summer programs or activities you planned during your Christmas break.

Investigate programs that still have space available or new ones that have appeared since you last researched. Establish healthy habits now by planning a physical workout routine over the summer or attend a physical activity camp or program. Consider a part-time summer job as another option and start your search now because many openings will be filled as it gets closer to the summer.

END OF SCHOOL YEAR

Transcript

Before school lets out, request an official copy of your transcript that includes grades from the final semester of junior year. You should not wait until school is over because counselors may not be available over the summer break to fulfill requests. Once you have the transcript, review it very carefully for any mistakes or omissions. You want to ensure its accuracy before actually submitting your college applications. While an unofficial copy of your transcript may suffice in most cases, I recommend an official version because it is possible that there will be discrepancies between the two.

SUMMER BREAK

ACT/SAT Prep

If you are planning to take the ACT or SAT this fall, then this summer you want to:

- » Review the previous sections in this book for test prep tips.
- » Complete several timed practice test sections.
- » Take an entire practice test at least once, simulating the timing for an official test.

Before The Application

- » Practice the strategies for tackling the different styles of questions in each section.
- » Brush up on any skills you are weak at or may have forgotten, especially in math.

If you are just starting your prep for the ACT or SAT, you need to review all of the previous ACT/SAT sections throughout this book to help you prepare. The amount of prep work required varies by individual ability. My ACT/SAT prep approach is based on the principle that it takes a commitment over time to achieve scores at your highest level of potential. Still, *any* amount of practice and exposure will increase your scoring potential.

Special Note: The ACT introduced a new option in the fall of 2020 called Section Retesting. After already completing a full test session, you can now retake individual ACT test sections without sitting for the entire test. I am excited about this new approach because it does have some advantages, but it is too new to fully grasp the impact of this change. **Before deciding to use this new option, be sure to check with the colleges where you plan to submit an application to make sure they will accept these scores.** Colleges that do not accept superscoring* will likely not allow Section Retesting.

---

* *Superscoring is the total of your highest scores on each test section from multiple test dates.*

College Tours

If you still need to explore your options, summer is another great time to go on college tours, especially near the beginning of the summer. There is an advantage to visiting colleges in the spring while classes are in session and students are on campus. On the other hand, the benefit of going now is that you may have a better idea of potential colleges, and you do not have the distraction of schoolwork. As you plan, review all of the previous sections regarding tours to get the most bang for your buck during these visits.

Don not forget to take pictures while on your visit, post them on your social media, and tag the school.

Summer Programs or Activities—Additional Ideas

If you have available time this summer, you can still take positive steps towards building your college application profile by participating in a summer program or enrichment activity. Keep in mind some of the ideas that I shared for prior summers:

- » READ!!! Find a couple of fun books to read over the summer. Many colleges ask, "What is one of your favorite books and why?" You can visit my website at *woolfolkworks.com/readinglist* for book recommendations.
- » Do volunteer work.
- » Research online or virtual classes that may still be available.
- » Use online resources to learn a new skill.
- » Plan to create a new club at your school. This type of endeavor can be fun, especially when done with a friend or two.
- » Develop a plan to address a problem in your school or community.
- » Create your own work opportunity (such as mowing lawns or babysitting).
- » Commit to a physical workout plan.

Do not worry about having too much time on your hands this summer because this is where the college application fun (and busyness) begins!

Before The Application

Mental Health

Julia Says

This is your last summer to do some kind of volunteer work, summer program, or internship that can be used in your college application. It is essential that you do something. When taking your mental health into consideration, this is where it actually gets fun. You get to decide what you want to do. If you have discovered that you love to dance, do a dance intensive, or if you are into law, intern at a firm. The beauty is that it is your choice, so go for something that will be great for your application but is also something you enjoy. Pick something tailored to you and your timeline. If you know that you do not have the mental capacity to do a particular activity consecutively for more than two weeks, do your best to find an activity based around your strengths and limitations. Take into consideration how much you can mentally handle so that you do not overwork yourself, because there is something important that should also be on your mind this summer.

*You must prioritize preparing for the college application process this summer. Trust me, I was really stressed out by my schoolwork and leadership positions that application deadlines and retaking the SAT made everything worse. All of that pressure was terrible for my mental health, and it was self-inflicted because I did not set a plan walking into it. For the sake of your future mental wellness, take this time to think about where you will apply, go on college tours, and also take the SAT and/or ACT. This will help give you a sense of direction so that you are not scrambling to apply everywhere and anywhere with no aim. Do your future self a favor and **please** take this time to prepare so you can avoid unnecessary stress.*

The College Application

The college application process needs to start this summer! All of your work and commitment over the last three years have led to this point. If you are applying to more than just a couple of schools, the college application process may make you feel like you have a part-time job for the next few months. You will pay the price later if you do not get a head start on your college application process. Waiting until school starts to begin is the worst mistake seniors make when applying to college. Therefore, this is the most detailed timeline in this book.

It is very disheartening to witness the stress level of students during the fall of their senior year as they attempt to navigate the difficulty of classwork along with the demands of completing applications. It is easy to underestimate how much time and work goes into tracking, collecting, and submitting all of the moving pieces. Organization and planning help this process go much more smoothly, especially if you have done all the prep work I have laid out for you in prior years. Deadlines will approach more quickly than you expect, especially when competing for scholarships. Do not allow laziness or complacency to stand between you and your dream school or scholarships!

Application Prep

This chapter is designed to prepare you for the actual college application process. Doing this prep work will make the process of filling out your

Before The Application

applications flow much more smoothly. Your goal is to complete every action item throughout this chapter before you go back to school in the fall.

As a reminder, the scope of this book is to put you in a position to be as attractive as possible to your target and stretch schools, and to be in strong competition for scholarships for at least your safe schools. There are many resources available that will guide you step by step through the actual application and college admissions processes, so take advantage of those resources for the tips and strategies needed for when you are physically completing applications. What I will do is help you to stay organized throughout the application process and assist in your time management of the action items and deadlines. This chapter will help you understand the purpose behind various sections of the application and the value that you need to convey through them in order to fully promote yourself.

From this point forward, be sure to consistently use the email account you created specifically for college admissions and check for emails daily. Skim every email you are sent, unless it is from a college you simply have no interest in. "You never know ¯_(ツ)_/¯." reviewing every email may potentially present you with a wonderful opportunity.

College Major Research

Colleges do not simply accept students that are the best fit for their university, since they **have to make sure that they have enough space to handle all of the majors across the student applications**. So, take researching your college major seriously because you want to choose a college that has solid programs in your potential field(s) of interest. In addition, you want to be prepared for the colleges that require you to provide your intended major on your application.

If you are like the average student and have not yet determined your college major, I encourage you to work towards finding two career fields of interest to help you get there. A field of interest will be along the lines of engineering, philosophy, healthcare, business, etc. Investigate various careers in the fields you choose to see which ones may interest you. Remember the value of interviewing actual professionals to learn in-depth details about their careers (please refer back to the College Majors section in the freshman chapter). This is a useful exercise even for those who have already picked a major. There are so many careers within a single discipline that we are too often drawn to a popular career role while unaware of others that may be a better fit. We can even dismiss a discipline altogether simply because we are put off by the dominant career in that field!

My son Christopher enjoyed political science from a very young age and eventually chose that as his major in college, even though he had no idea what he would choose as a career. The one thing he was adamant about was not wanting to be an attorney because the only vision he had of this career field was of trial lawyers. While in college, he discovered various career paths within the field of law, and fast forward to today—he just graduated from The University of Texas School of Law, the 14th ranked law school in the country.

After choosing a few career fields that you are interested in, or even if you already know what you wish to major in, complete the following steps:

1. Compile a list of college majors that lead towards these career fields.
2. Find colleges that are known for these majors using websites like *princetonreview.com* and *mycollegeoptions.org*.
3. Confirm that the schools already in your college interest pool offer the majors in the list you just created.
4. Search the websites of colleges in your interest pool and read the overviews of the majors on your list.
5. Find specific careers that align with each major. Many college websites provide a list of potential careers for the majors they offer.

Before The Application

Special Note: Step #2 led to a great opportunity for my youngest son. Aaron was always interested in studying computer science, computer engineering, or math, so he was highly interested in Georgia Institute of Technology and MIT. When researching colleges best known for his intended majors, he came across Harvey Mudd College (ranked #3 in computer science by *U.S. News*). Unless you are from the West Coast, you probably have not heard of this school located in California. After learning more about this liberal arts college known for their strong programs in math, science, and engineering, Aaron became quite interested in Harvey Mudd. He was eventually accepted and received a nice scholarship offer. However, after serious consideration, better scholarship offers took Harvey Mudd out of contention.

College Major Course Requirements

Once you have compiled a list of potential college majors and picked a few prospective schools that have a good reputation for that major, review their websites and find all the required courses to complete that major. The inability to succeed in a required course is a significant reason why students change majors in college. Too often, students do not understand course requirements until they have already committed to a college and a major. Take into consideration whether a potential major requires taking courses in an area that you struggle with before committing.

Here are some potential benefits for researching course requirements for your intended major at each college to which you intend to apply:

- » Knowing which colleges have required courses which you should avoid for your own interest
- » Knowing requirement differences between similar majors may help you make the better choice

» Knowing that if all colleges require a very difficult set of courses, maybe you need to reevaluate your intended major

This may be an extreme example, but imagine a student choosing to attend their dream school of Georgia Tech to become a biomedical engineer as their gateway into the healthcare field. They send in a deposit and then turn down all other scholarship offers. Upon meeting with their advisor, they learn that this major requires two levels of calculus and two levels of physics—courses they barely survived on the high school level. After realizing this, they remember that they had a scholarship for Emory University to major in Biology, where there was no physics requirement and they only needed to take a life science calculus class. But now that it is well beyond the college decision deadline, this opportunity, along with all of their other college choices, is no longer available.

College Application Pool

Recall that your College Interest Pool is a list of all the colleges you expressed interest in. Each college should have at least one reason for why they are on the list. Before the end of the summer, pare your College Interest Pool down to a College Application Pool, which is a list of schools you plan on applying to. Once you decide on this list, you will add each school to your College Tracking Spreadsheet and fill in each of the fields. This is not the final list of colleges that you will actually apply to, as you will likely opt to add or eliminate a school or two over the next few months.

My rule of thumb is that your College Application Pool should be about 30% larger than the total number of schools to which you will eventually submit an application but should not exceed double. This means you need to have an idea of the total number of schools you plan on applying to. I believe a good number to shoot for is nine colleges (give or take two):

- » Three safe schools—colleges you feel 95% certain that you can get into and at least one is a clear financial fit. These may not be your top choice, but they satisfy your requirements for the next level.
- » Three to four target schools—colleges you believe you have a decent chance to get into with a potential financial fit. These are schools you prefer to attend and have benefits that extend beyond meeting your requirements.
- » Three to four stretch schools—colleges that are a stretch to gain acceptance to but can provide an added bonus if you are able to attend.

(If you use nine as your final number of actual college applications, your College Application Pool should have between twelve to eighteen schools.)

While I suggest about nine as the total number of schools to submit an actual application to, every situation is unique and will be influenced by personal preferences and constraints. Here are a few reasons to adjust your final number:

- » Applying to fewer schools is recommended when you have a high probability for admittance to your primary school choices and the financial side of the college decision is understood well in advance of the college application season.
- » If being awarded a merit scholarship is a major component in your enrollment decision, consider adding more schools that offer college-sponsored scholarships. In this scenario, it is good to cast a wider net.
- » If you have a very strong desire to attend a school on your stretch or target level, you should consider increasing the number of schools you apply to in that specific category.

Special Note: I did have one particular rule for my children that I hope you are willing to follow: only apply to colleges that you are willing to attend! Competition or camaraderie with your peers should not be a catalyst to where you apply. I have a hard time understanding why students apply to colleges that they have no intention of attending, especially when they secure scholarships that they know they would never accept. Of course, there is an exception to every rule. For example, even if you know you cannot attend your dream college (usually because of cost), I understand you would still like to know if you will be accepted.

Eventually you will need to decide on the final list of schools to which you will apply. Details from the College Tracking Spreadsheet and the requirements on the actual applications may influence your decision. You can use online tools like Parchment or College Vine to calculate the likelihood of being accepted into various colleges based on your current profile. This may help you determine if a school is a target school versus a safe school. You can also find similar websites that are designed to help you find schools of "best fit" based on your preferences, such as Niche or Unigo.

An obvious hurdle when applying to more than a few colleges are the accompanying application fees, ACT/SAT score reporting fees, and possibly financial aid fees (CSS Profile). I believe that colleges must have application fees to manage the number of application submissions each year. If there were no costs associated with applying to college, many students would submit 50-100 applications and college admissions officers would be completely overwhelmed.

If you have a *legitimate* financial need, there are ways to obtain an application fee waiver*:

» Ask your professional school counselor for fee waivers.
» See your local high school counselor for assistance if you are home-schooled (ACT/SAT fee waivers should serve as a basis for application fee waivers).

Before The Application

- » Ask for a waiver while on campus visits (this is a long shot but worth the try).
- » Check if individual schools waive fees for applying online.
- * *The majority of students applying to college would like to avoid paying fees, so you must be able to demonstrate need to obtain a fee waiver.*

Financial Package

Which schools can you afford to attend? Most people think the answer is simply knowing the estimated cost of attendance minus any likely scholarships, followed by the hope for any available financial aid. Instead, you should understand the difference between these two questions:

"How much does it cost to attend _____ University?"
versus
"How much will it cost **me** to attend _____ University?"

Many families cannot answer these questions because they do not understand how financial aid works at schools like Yale or Northwestern compared to how it works at schools like Georgetown or a local state university. Here are some examples that show why it is important to research the financial aid packages of all colleges independently:

- » The University of Texas utilizes competitive recruitment and offers scholarship packages to make the university an attractive option for high-potential students, regardless of income.
- » **They only provide a limited number of scholarships, with no guarantee that every student will receive one.**
- » Georgetown University meets the *full demonstrated financial need* of every admitted student, <u>but students may be required to take out federal student loans</u> as part of their financial aid awards. **Georgetown expects a minimum student contribution of**

$2,200 to $2,800 per year regardless of your income (as of 2020). After Georgetown calculates the family's financial responsibility, the student must utilize their FAFSA-calculated federal loans and Federal Work Study amounts before the school will apply any grants and need-based scholarships to cover the rest of the balance.

» Harvard and Stanford meet the *full demonstrated financial need* of every admitted student, and students are not required to take out student loans as part of their financial aid awards.

» Harvard has an endowment that allows them to offer a generous need-based financial aid program. **For families with an annual income below $65,000, the expected contribution is zero! Families with an annual income between $65,000 and $150,000 will contribute between 0 and 10 percent of their income** (as of 2020).

Many of the top-rated private schools in the country offer financial packages similar to Harvard and Stanford, and this is one of the major motivations for this book.* If you are outstanding in and outside of the classroom, I want your hard work to pay off so that there is a good chance that you can affordably attend any dream school of your choice. Unfortunately, there are many capable students in America that simply do not have the privilege of understanding how to build a fully developed college profile for an exceptional college application.

* *The message in the previous paragraph is geared more towards the top 1-5% of the students in the country. To be clear, this book is designed for* **all** *college-bound students. Ivy League colleges and their peers are not the only roads to success. Your grit will carry you forward to your destination regardless of the path you take to get there.*

The differences in financial aid offerings among colleges are important to understand when it is time to finalize your college

Before The Application

application list. The correlation between your circumstances and your estimated financial aid package at a college can increase or decrease the number of schools in your College Application Pool.

> **Parents**: Please do not wait until college acceptance letters are received and financial aid packages are awarded to start determining what is affordable for your family. I encourage you to have conversations with your child now to discuss what is feasible and what is out of range. Visit *studentaid.gov* where you can use their tool "Estimate Your Aid (FAFSA4caster)" so that your family will have an idea of what you are getting into. In addition, visit the financial aid websites of any schools that you are set on applying to for a total cost estimation specific to each school.

Join College Forums?

There are college community forums categorized by school that provide advice designed for students and/or parents (e.g. *CollegeConfidential.com* and *back2college.com*). There are pros and cons to joining and participating in these forums.

Pros:
» These forums can serve as valuable resources for gaining insight into specific colleges or programs from families that have been through the process before you.
» You can ask questions that are specific to your concerns.
» You can search for (virtually) any topic and you will most likely find a previous thread addressing it.
» You can learn about special programs and scholarship opportunities.
» You can gain a better understanding of clubs and organizations and many other topics.

Cons:
» You can get biased perspectives based on isolated experiences and unpopular opinions that can dissuade you from attending a school or pursuing opportunities.
» You may run into people who simply want to brag about their success.
» When decision letters start rolling in, it can be stressful and discouraging when other students/families are posting their acceptances into schools and scholarship programs that you are still waiting to hear back from.

I believe that forums can serve as a good resource for gathering information about colleges and related programs, but use them with caution, vet all information, and put advice into proper perspective.

High School Resumé

As a freshman, you were urged to write a resumé as if it were the end of your senior year. At that time, you likely could not imagine what your story would look like at this point. As a sophomore, you were encouraged to start your actual resumé and then add to it as time went along. Now is the time to polish your resumé and make sure it is up to date.

A resumé should speak to your accomplishments and to your brand. You want the reader to see your awards and honors as well as get a glimpse of what has mattered most to you. Just like college applications, most resumés are read by people who do not know you, so use this as an opportunity to convey what you want them to think about you. But it is not just the content of your resumé that tells your story.

Contrary to the old adage, "never judge a book by its cover," most people are visually influenced. We determine what we spend our money on more by what something looks like rather than its true quality. When a resumé is well-organized with a great visual appeal, the perceived quality of its content is elevated. The opposite is true as well: a poorly formatted resumé can greatly undermine the content. Similar to the format, a poorly written resumé portrays a negative image of the individual. However, an easy-to-read resumé with no grammar or spelling errors makes the content seem more legitimate.

If you have not yet started your resumé or want/need to make improvements, you should:

1. Conduct extensive research on resumé styles.
2. Select a style that fits your personality (there are many free templates available).
3. Customize it to tell your story.
4. Make sure that every detail you include provides value to the reader.
5. Prioritize your resumé so that the most important information is presented first.

No matter what, **do *not* put false information on your resumé!** If (and when) the lie is discovered, it will negate all the positive things you have done and likely remove you from consideration for college admission or a scholarship award. No matter how small the lie, it is just not worth it!

Application Warning

It was literally the eleventh hour as Brian feverishly worked to complete his application to the University of Southern California. He submitted the application with less than an hour remaining before the deadline. The panic was not due to a lack of planning nor procrastination; hours before he had completed the majority of the application online when everything went away unexpectedly!

The lesson is: ***never fill out an application directly in an online portal!*** Every college and scholarship application question/essay should be written and saved in an outside document until it is ready to be transferred to the actual application online. You may wish to take it a step further and save your documents locally (and in the cloud) so that you will have a backup and can access them anywhere.

Early Action and Early Decision

Some colleges offer the opportunity to submit an application early (in the fall) before their regular application deadline (typically in January or February). You will receive an admission decision from the college well in advance of the usual notification date. You should only consider these programs if you know that you are a strong candidate for admissions (based on ACT/SAT scores, GPA, and class rank). If you believe your application will be aided by a boost to your GPA with a strong showing from your first semester grades, it may be best to wait until the regular deadline to submit your application.

What are your options?—A college will either offer Early Decision or Early Action (some offer both).

- » **Early Decision** (ED) is a ***binding*** process which means that if you are accepted, you are ***financially*** obligated to attend that college and withdraw applications from all other schools. Also, you cannot apply to any other colleges early.
- » **Early Action** (EA) is a ***non-binding*** process which means you are not obligated to attend if you are accepted. The advantage is that you can usually apply early to multiple colleges and can compare financial packages from multiple schools before making a commitment (including regular decision acceptances).

» **Single-choice Early Action** is the same as EA except applicants cannot apply early to any other college.

When should you consider using either of these options?—You should only choose ED when you are 100% certain that you are applying to your best-fit college and are able to accept the financial obligation. Only consider EA if you are certain that you have put together a strong application and essay. In either case, making this decision means you have already committed to doing a lot of research before the fall of your senior year.

What are the advantages?

» Shows you are serious about attending a school, which *may* give you a leg up.
» If accepted:
» Can cut down on the stress of completing a lot of applications and waiting on decision day.
» Saves the time and cost of submitting multiple applications.

There is no singular approach for choosing whether to apply to colleges early. Just be sure that you match *all* the criteria before opting to choose ED. Also note that some colleges have early deadlines to be considered for major scholarships that may or may not be tied to EA or ED.

Activities/Programs/Awards/Honors Descriptions

After having several off-the-record conversations with admissions officers, I have concluded that colleges want game-changers: students who will eventually change the world and carry their college name along with them. Your chance to show them that you are that student comes when college applications require you to list your activities along with your awards and honors. **Your ability to market your leadership, passions, strong interests, and community service can give you a chance for your stretch schools and put you at the head of the pack for your target schools.**

You already have a document that lists all your activities, programs, awards, and honors with dates, names, a description, and value statements. The Common App and the Coalition App provide limited space to describe each activity, so tailor your descriptions to fit the character limits below (as of 2019-2020):

The Common App
» Activities (up to 10)
  › Position/Leadership and Organization Name—50 characters
  › Activity Description—150 characters
» Awards & Honors (up to 5)
  › Honor or Award Title—100 characters

The Coalition App
» Activities (up to 8)
  › Activity Name—64 characters
  › Activity Description—255 characters
» Awards & Honors (up to 5)
  › Honor or Award Title—255 characters

For each of your activities, honors, and awards, write two descriptions: one following the Common App limits and one following the Coalition App limits. Some colleges only use one portal, but many use both. If a college appears on both portals, the difference in limits may influence which one you choose to apply through. You may want the luxury of the two extra activity sections offered by Common App or the larger character limit offered by the Coalition App.

Before The Application

When you describe an activity or program, your goal is to advertise your brand. Most of the activities that you list should promote a least one of the following (hopefully you have at least one activity for each category):

» Demonstrated passion and/or dedication to an interest
» Impactful leadership
» Meaningful influence with community service

As you write out your description, do *not* provide an overview of the organization or program. To make sure that including it has value, tell the personal impact you made while part of the organization, doing the activity, or attending the program. If you have an activity that is worth including but does not have a strong impact, consider using it to send a short message about who you are by revealing something that you care about or illustrating what makes you unique.

I once chaperoned a group of high school teens on a trip to a Navajo mission school in Show Low, Arizona. It was worth it when a student listed this community service on their application because it showed a willingness to selflessly aid people who were different from him. Only stating that they "spent the week fixing up the grounds" adds little additional value. Including how it led to "an interest in the preservation of marginalized cultures" provides a little insight into his values as an individual.

For the program, activity, award, or honor where you had the most impact, write a brief summary (not restricted by the above character limits) that demonstrates your passion or strong interest. Do the same for one that exemplifies your success as a leader. These will be useful for questions on scholarship applications and additional questions from individual colleges.

There are many websites offering even more advice on how to fill out this section of the application, such as what type of activities to include and how to effectively word your descriptions. For example, Easywise's article "15 Mistakes to Avoid on the Common App 'Activities' Section" provides many valuable tips. Feel free to take advantage of these additional resources.

Common and Coalition Apps

Create an account for both the Common App and the Coalition for College App using the email account you created specifically for college admissions. Browse both apps to become familiar with how to navigate their layouts. Both sites provide guides and tutorials that are worth reviewing. Take the time to understand all the requirements necessary to complete the application, especially the process for requesting recommendations. The cores of these shared portals are made up of seven basic sections (Coalition App breaks the sections down into smaller segments but incorporate the same information):

1. Profile—contact information, demographics, citizenship, etc.
2. Family—information about people living in your household including siblings already in college
3. Education—high school details, class size, counselor info, GPA, etc.
4. Testing—self-reported scores on SAT, ACT, AP exam(s), IB exam(s), etc.
5. Courses & Grades—self-reported list of ALL courses taken while in high school along with grades; courses planned for senior year (this is why you should get your transcript at the end of your junior year)
6. Activities—activities, programs, awards, and honors
7. Writing—the magic essay

Most of the core parts of the application can be filled out right away, and sections 1-5 can all be done in a day. Although you will be self-reporting your grades and ACT/SAT scores, report them accurately because you will still have to send in the official records (in most cases directly to the schools).

After you finish reviewing the core sections, pick at least one college that you feel pretty confident that you will be applying to in each portal (or just pick one randomly), and select it to have an idea of what a college may list for additional requirements. Each school will require some number of teacher recommendations, but whether you have to provide short answer responses, additional essays, supporting documents, or a portfolio will depend on the specific school and your major.

As soon as you complete the Activities, Programs, Awards, & Honors descriptions (from the previous section), I suggest that you go ahead and add them to your application(s). Take your time and ensure that you present your best brand. Prioritize the order that your items appear by starting with the most important ones first. You will also be asked for the amount of time spent on each activity, which you should have documented in your Activity Log. Be purposeful in filling out your application; do not rush through just to get it done.

The great value in knowing what is expected of you is that you will understand the scope of the work ahead of you. Now that you know what is in store, you should appreciate why starting now will prevent a lot of stress in a few short months. My advice is to take advantage of the ample time you have this summer by trying to complete at least sections 1 through 5. I do not want you scrambling to complete your application towards the end of the next semester; let those who procrastinate stress over not producing their best application.

College Essay

The college essay can make or break you. Sorry to be so blunt, but it is better to know and properly prepare than to downplay it and miss out on getting it right. For many college applicants, the essay is the most difficult part of the application. It seems like it should not be too difficult for a college-bound senior to write a 600-word essay on a topic of their choice, but this essay may be more challenging than you realize. It is imperative that you invest whatever amount of time is required to nail it.

Figuring out your approach to writing the essay should not be taken lightly. You must first decide which prompt you will respond to and then determine what message you want to convey and how you want to express it. Not giving the essay the proper time and attention can be the difference between "Congratulations!" and "We regret to inform you…." A poor essay may cause an admissions officer to believe that you were not willing to get the assistance you needed, you did not commit the necessary time, or you simply did not care enough. I highly recommend that you take advantage of any and every resource that can assist you with writing and perfecting your essay.

Based on our experiences, here are some strategies that you may find helpful:

» While there is no single approach to writing your essay and no "right way" it should look, there are things you want to avoid:
  › **Do not use your essay to merely repeat your resume.** Admissions officers want to learn about who you are, not read a brag sheet of your awards and accomplishments. However, you can still reference other parts of your application as long as the main focus is on revealing something about your life or personality.
  › **Do not blindly accept any one person's advice on your essay.** Take all advice into consideration because if multiple people you trust advise you against an aspect of your essay, you may need to put your ego aside and rethink your approach.
  › **Do not submit an essay without it being properly vetted.** I suggest that you have at least three capable

Before The Application

people review it because your inherent bias of what you like and believe to be correct means that you will not be able to identify all of your mistakes. In addition, do not rely on editing software because it is prone to mistakes, cannot discern the intentions behind your words, and will strip your personality from the essay. The end goal is for your essay to be beautifully written with NO errors.

» Your essay should capture the reader's attention from the beginning and hold onto it. It does not have to be the most amazing essay ever written, but it should definitely be engaging.

» While it is great to present a perfectly written essay, you will completely miss the mark if that is all you have. **The actual value of a great essay comes from being able to portray what you want an admissions officers to learn about you and how well you tell your story.**

» This essay can be approached as a personal statement, similar to what is required for graduate or professional school applications. Researching strategies or reading samples may give you ideas on how to approach your essay. You can find '12 Great Personal Statement Examples For College Applications' on The College Essay Guy website.

» If it fits within your story, you can make an impact by telling the reader something unique that they can associate with you. This can be accomplished if the "theme" of your essay is uncommon or by including a rare fact about you within the essay.

I have reviewed some very well-written essays that left me impressed with the students' writing skills, but I unfortunately learned absolutely nothing about who they were. This is a common problem I have heard in my conversations with admissions officers. They want to learn more about you than your ability to craft a well-written essay, and they want to learn more than what is already in your application. Do your homework, get tips on how to approach your essay, make it your own, and tell your story.

The official prompts for college essays are typically released in the summer, no later than July 1st. The prompts for the Common and Coalition applications rarely change much from year to year. Before school starts, you should read over the essay prompts and begin to narrow down the list to the ones you are interested in writing about. The shared college application portals have always had a generic prompt that allows you the freedom to choose your topic, but one of the other prompts may be better suited for you. I suggest that you decide on at least three prompts and then jot down ideas of what you could write about for each one. This exercise may help you determine which prompt is the best fit.

Supplemental Essays/Questions

The total number of essays you will write during the college application season will quickly add up. Along with your main college essay, you will likely be asked to write other shorter essays for:

- » Individual colleges on the Common/Coalition App
- » Honors colleges
- » Independent college application platforms
- » Scholarships
- » Special college programs

I would estimate that the average student can expect to write over twenty essays of varying sizes during the college application season. I will let you in on a little hint—whether they are short, medium, or long, most essays you write will just be versions of three to five different essays. For my kids, each college application season probably yielded 40 to 50 essays or question responses that were all variations of four or five distinct essays.

Essay Length

Every college or scholarship essay prompt will come with a word count recommendation or limit. The wrong number of words in your essay can leave a negative impression, and in some cases can even remove you from consideration. **You must stay within the word or letter count requirements for the essay.** Unless the instructions specifically state otherwise, consider all minimum and maximum counts as hard limits with no exceptions. Even when staying within the limits provided, your final word count is also important. You do not want to submit too short of an essay. Here are a few of my guidelines regarding how to target your final word count based on the essay requirements:

Word Limit	Word Count Guidelines	
	Bare Minimum	Ideal Minimum
250–650 (Common App)	500	525
None (Coalition)	500	525
800	600	675
500	375	400
250	175	200

Let your final word count be determined by your message. Every sentence should bring value to the purpose of your essay. If you are able to fully express your message and are above the minimum word count guidelines, do not feel obligated to get close to the maximum word limit. Avoid filler sections in your writing; unnecessary "fluff" undermines your essay's ability to hold the attention of a reader. If you are struggling to reach the minimum count, take a step back and examine the message you are trying to convey or determine if you have enough substance to support your message. **Avoid using contractions in your essay** even when attempting to get your word count below the limit.

The Coalition App lifted its restrictions on the essay but recommends 500-550 words. I suggest 525-575 words as a good range with a limit of 650 for most essays. There are legitimate situations where going well over 650 words can be justified, but long essays are always a risk. Admissions officers have hundreds of essays to read, *so make sure a longer essay is well worth the read.*

Interview Strategies

Over the next year, you may be required to participate in a college or scholarship interview. Most college admissions interviews held on campus are conducted by the admissions staff, while the ones held near your home are conducted by a local alumnus. While scholarship interviews are a significant part of the decision process, college admissions interviews do not usually carry major weight *unless* you truly impress the interviewer or set off an alarm. Yet, I encourage you to take advantage of any admissions interview opportunity because it demonstrates your serious interest in a school.

Interviews are more of an art than a hard science. Here are a few tips that I suggest you practice in preparation for any interview:

» **Be respectful**—Arrive to your appointment well ahead of time and be sure to give plenty of advance notice if your plans change.
» **Be presentable**—Your grooming and attire must be neat and clean. If provided, be sure to follow any dress code guidelines. If no instructions are given, either ask or go with the default of business casual attire.
» **Be polite**—Start with a smile and follow their lead with the greeting. Do not force anyone into a handshake if they do not offer their hand first.
» **Be yourself**—Well, be the best version of yourself. Do not try

to change who you are to become who you think they want you to be.
- » **Be present**—You must show that you want to be there by not thinking about other things going on in your life.
- » **Be relatable**—You must be willing to be engaging. By the end of a great interview, you should have bonded with the interviewer in some way.
- » **Be aware**—"Know thyself" sounds fairly simple but many people struggle with confidently speaking about themselves.
- » **Be honest**—Do not lie for any reason. Being caught in a lie will discredit any (and all) good you have done. Omission is fair game as long as you were not asked a direct question or it is not used to deceive (because that is the same as telling a lie).
- » **Be positive**—Avoid negative responses as much as possible. If you must say something negative, follow it up with what you learned from it, how you grew from it, and/or how you will handle it better in the future.
- » **Be patient**—Do not feel like you need to rush to respond to a question. It is okay to pause for a *few seconds* to gather your thoughts before speaking. If you tend to speak fast, be sure to slow down and enunciate as you talk.
- » **Be thoughtful**—The purpose of every question is for them to learn something about you. Consider why you are being asked a question before you answer. If they ask for you to "describe a time you worked on a group project that went wrong," do not admit that you hate working with other people. Instead, tell them what you did to get a positive outcome. (This is a proper use of omission).
- » **Be prepared**—Do your homework. Know detailed information about the school, scholarship, program, or job. and be ready to ask a question or two. Also use this information to be ready for any questions that require specific facts about the organization or institution.

» **Be ready**—As a hiring manager, I have conducted interviews where I truly believe that the applicant was surprised to actually be asked questions. Make sure you are prepared to answer any interview question.
    › Anticipate the questions you may be asked. College admissions interviewers will ask different questions from scholarship or job interviewers. A blog post on The Prep Scholar website, "The 14 College Interview Questions You Must Prepare For," does an excellent job of presenting potential questions asked in a college admissions interview.
    › There is one question you must prepare for as you are almost certain to be asked one of its variants: **"Tell me a little bit about yourself."** This may be the toughest interview question there is, and your response will require some forethought. Use this as your chance to tell the interviewer something about yourself that you really want them to walk away with. Tell them who you are versus what you do. I caution against using this as an opportunity to simply rehash your resumé.
    › Many interviewers utilize situational questions to learn about the behavior of candidates in certain circumstances, such as "Tell me about a time you worked on a group project that did not go as planned." Be sure to practice how to properly respond. One tactic is to use the STAR method:
        • **Situation**: Set the scene and give the necessary details of your example.
        • **Task**: Describe what your responsibility was in that situation.
        • **Action**: Explain exactly what steps you took to address the situation.
        • **Result**: Share what outcomes your actions achieved.

Social Media Footprint

Do another review of your social media accounts and consider removing any inappropriate or offensive material from your online footprint. Things that you may find funny or innocent need to be examined to ensure others will not find them offensive. You should stay true to who you are and what you believe in, but understand that there is always a chance that there could be consequences to expressing certain views.

Here are some actions summarized from Veritas Prep that you may want to consider adopting during the college application and scholarship season:

- » Change your profile picture to make a good first impression
- » Follow the social media accounts of schools you are interested in
- » Follow the social media accounts of your high school including clubs/organization you are in
- » Choose your interests wisely and avoid "liking" things that could be viewed negatively by a college
- » Try to keep your social posts positive
- » Ask friends and family members to refrain from tagging you in photos that could put you in a negative light
- » *Remember: you can always remove tags if necessary.*
- » Remove unfriendly comments on your posts because allowing them signifies your approval
- » Ensure that everything on your account is legal

If taking the steps to have a positive profile is too much work for you, consider changing your username to something not easily identifiable and set it to private. This does not guarantee protection, but it at least makes it much more difficult to find you.

Twelfth Grade— Finishing Strong

You must remain focused in hopes to avoid living with regret!

"What kind of competitor sees the finish line and slows down… always finish strong!"
–Gary Ryan Blair

Note: If you are first reading this book as a senior, I highly recommend that you go back and read the "The College Application" chapter in its entirety.

If finishing high school is all you ever want to accomplish in life, now is the time to relax and coast to graduation. Otherwise, take this school year as seriously as any other. Stay organized and stick to your plan, even if it has to adjust as you progress forward.

This chapter is a model for the senior year wheel needed to "drive off" towards college success. Our objective is to:

» Appreciate the value of **reading** at the next level
» Utilize one last tip for **ACT/SAT prep**
» Realize the importance of **finishing strong**
» Make sure you keep up with your **college correspondence**

Before The Application

- » Perform action items for handling the application season:
  - › Properly manage your letters of recommendation
  - › Organize and complete your applications
  - › Create an impactful college essay
  - › Complete your financial aid paperwork
  - › Manage all applications through your tracking spreadsheet or app
  - › Stay on top of scholarship opportunities
  - › Submit your transcript for admissions, mid-year reports, and final transcript
  - › Prepare for your admissions notifications
  - › Analyze your final college decision
  - › Express gratitude and look forward
  - › Become familiar with your new college

Senior Focus Point: Senior year should be one of the most memorable times of your life. Be sure to enjoy the moment and not allow your hectic schedule to keep you from the joys of your youth. Many of your classmates will suffer from the infamous "senioritis" and slack off for much of senior year. Other peers will be so busy trying to stay on top of schoolwork and college applications that they will have no time for social interaction for a good part of their senior year. A key part of life is learning how to find balance and properly prioritize. Organization and planning are the tools that will allow you to manage your work life along with your social life.

Education has a purpose, and that purpose is not defined by a letter grade. Every college-bound student should understand the value of an education, appreciate the opportunity to expand their knowledge base, and want to be in school to learn. As a senior, you should be taking several college prep courses. These classes are called "college prep" for a reason. The more you learn the course material now, the better prepared you will be for the rigor of college. You are in a position of learning for no other reason than your own goals, so your actions will either *help you* or *hurt you*. Therefore, be wise and make decisions with a purpose; do not live life by happenstance.

Julia Says

You made it! You are finally a senior. I am sure you are ready to graduate at this moment and so are the rest of your classmates. This is why it is even more important to be mentally set on following through with your academic, extracurricular, college application, and mental wellness responsibilities. The first step is knowing what you are walking into now that you are a senior. Your first semester will likely be your toughest because you have to juggle schoolwork, activities, personal essays, and college applications. Naturally, all of these factors can affect your mental health in different ways. They can overwhelm you to the point that you spiral or decide to slack off in the name of mental health. "Senioritis" is what can affect students most mentally, because it gives them the feeling of, "I'm so close to the finish line that I don't have to do anything else." But when it is time for transcripts and to write about yourself for college applications, seniors start stressing since they have the bare minimum to impress colleges with.

For the sake of your mental health and college success, you are going to have to utilize everything you have learned about yourself to manage these obligations. Even if you have not fully discovered yourself, you can stay mentally sane by having the right mindset throughout your first semester. If you walk in knowing the goals you want to achieve, you will also want to strive for the satisfaction of attaining them. Knowing that there is a light at the end of the tunnel will help push you through this semester. Once second semester comes around, you will truly be able to start to relax your mind from all of the hard work you put in over the past three and a half years.

Before The Application

The Fundamentals—Final Touches

Reading—A Way of Life

I truly hope reading has become part of your DNA. Some professors at the college level are known to do more facilitating than teaching. More of the responsibility for learning the content of your classes will fall on your shoulders, so improving your reading comprehension skills will help prepare you for this shift. It is not uncommon to regularly have large reading assignments, thus strong reading comprehension skills can help you avoid undue stress!

I have shared each of my son's favorite books to read as a teen in an effort to give you some recommendations to add to your library. Now that you are a senior, here is your opportunity to do the same for students reading this book after you. Go to my website and tell us your favorite book or series that you have read while in high school. We will compile a list and display it on our website for future students to see. Go to *woolfolkworks.com/favoritebook*.

Reading Check-In!

Did you complete your reading challenge?

I was able to finish _____ books over the last year

Reading should now be a way of life, so your **Commitment to Reading Challenge** has no end. Your challenge is simple:

I *will* commit to being a lifelong reader!
Sign here: _____

ACT/SAT Prep

If you plan on taking one of the college entrance exams during your senior year, be sure to consider the deadlines for your college applications when scheduling your test date. You will have early deadlines when applying to a college through Early Decision (ED) or Early Action (EA), and many scholarships offered by colleges also have early deadlines.

If you take any of these entrance exams multiple times, some colleges will allow for you to select which set of scores to send in and others will require that you send all scores from all tests taken. Colleges will be looking for a level of consistency between exams taken within months of each other and growth between tests taken further apart. So even if you are retaking a test primarily to improve your score in just one section, you still need to approach the test with the understanding that your total score matters. Basically, you must properly prepare for every test and always give your best effort.

Remember: The ACT now allows Section Retesting after already completing a full test session. This may be a good option at this time, but only after you have checked with the colleges where you are applying to ensure they will accept these scores.

Senior Essentials—Taking Care

Finish Strong

Most college application deadlines are in mid to late December or early to mid-January. Even if a college you plan to apply to has a later deadline, I encourage you to have the bulk of your applications submitted by mid-January. For most students, applications will be submitted with a transcript that includes courses through the end of your junior year. Before a decision is made, the grades from the first semester of your senior year WILL be assessed as part of your admission decision (unless you apply Early Decision or Action). I have watched seniors lose out on college opportunities simply because they relaxed their efforts.

College admission decisions are typically announced on April 1st, but acceptance is provisional pending the receipt of your final transcript. It is heartbreaking when a student has already secured a college acceptance only to have it withdrawn because they took school for granted their last semester of high school. Learning and preparing for college should be enough to override any urge to not finish your senior year strong, but at the very least the threat of having a college acceptance revoked should motivate you to care about midterm and final grades.

College Correspondence

During the college application season, you may receive a lot of email and standard mail correspondence from colleges. However much you may want to discard it all, take the time to read (or at least scan) each one. You never know where your best opportunity may come from. All of my kids ended up at schools that were not on their radar at the start of senior year due to the great opportunities that came their way.

> **Christopher**—By the end of the first semester of senior year, he had not even considered the three schools that offered him full scholarships.

> **Brian**—He originally envisioned attending an Ivy League school or Rice University, and then his focus went to attending the University of Southern California before making the decision to attend the University of Georgia. (He was accepted to an Ivy and received scholarships to attend each of the other schools.)

Aaron—He entered his senior year with the Massachusetts Institute of Technology (MIT) at the top of his list. In October, his initial visit to Clemson was cancelled due to a hurricane, so a last-minute trip was scheduled during his Thanksgiving break. The offer from Clemson was so nice that he chose this option over a full scholarship to the University of North Carolina and a full tuition scholarship to Vanderbilt University.

Stay flexible and keep your options open. Completely dismissing a school before a fair evaluation could keep you from a great situation. I talk about "dream schools" throughout this book, but our family focused more on a "dream scenario." A dream scenario for us meant:

- A *well-respected* university
- A *strong* reputation for intended major
- Meeting the environmental preferences of the child
- **An extremely attractive financial package**

Senior Timeline—Focus on the Details

BY END OF SEPTEMBER

Letters of Recommendation

Teachers—Though some undervalue its importance, the teacher recommendation is an important element in the decisions of college admissions officers. They want to see how excited each recommender is to write about you, to get a feel for the type of learner you are, to understand how well you interact with others in your class, and to learn about your unique characteristics. This is why it is important that the teacher who writes your recommendation actually knows you and can easily say great things about you. Otherwise you take the risk of a generic recommendation that can be harmful to your cause. **Be very intentional about which teachers you ask to write your letters of recommendation.**

Try to identify the teachers you want to request for a letter of recommendation early in the school year. Make your request in writing well before you need to provide them with any deadlines. Review your College Tracking spreadsheet to determine whether you need teachers from a specific subject. If you believe that a teacher in a subject area closely related to your intended college major will write you a good recommendation, you should prioritize them as a recommender. It is also a good idea to have a recommendation from a teacher whose discipline is different from your intended major to show your well-roundedness.

Counselors—Your professional school counselor is responsible for the following submissions concerning college applications:

- **High school transcript**—This is the initial transcript that you submit with your college application that only includes grades through your junior year.
- **Mid-year report and final-year report**—Colleges want to ensure that your trajectory in high school continues and that you finish strong, so they require an update of your grades from halfway through and at the end of your senior year.
- **Secondary school report**—This report places your academic experience in context by providing information such as:
    - The number of AP or IB courses offered at your school
    - Your academic strength in relation to the rest of your class
    - The percentage of students at your school who attended college in recent years
    - The economic makeup of your school/community

» **Counselor recommendation**—In addition to the standard information that is requested, some schools may ask for a recommendation from the counselor. This letter may include highlights of your special skills and personal involvement and convey how you go above and beyond to set yourself apart from other students. A recommendation allows your counselor to provide information about any special circumstances you may have faced in high school and how you contributed to the academic and social community. Even if the counselor recommendation is optional for a certain school, you may want to ask your counselor to submit one anyway. For example, a counselor elaborating on a special accomplishment in a recommendation may be another avenue for highlighting its significance.

Special Note: If your counselor cannot (or chooses not to) write a recommendation, or you have given them a reason for not writing a positive one, you may be able to take advantage of an "optional/other" recommendation in its stead. If you have a staff or faculty member (outside of one of your teachers) that you believe will speak highly of you and can convey your overall impact at the school, consider asking them to be a recommender. *I do caution you to use this option of replacing the counselor recommendation only when necessary.*

Our Strategy—This was our approach for handling recommendations that you can use as a guide.

Strategies for choosing recommenders:

» Established positive student-teacher relationships with them.
» Determined which teachers enjoyed having my sons as students and would be happy to write a letter for them.
» Selected one more teacher than the minimum required for an application. (Despite their good intentions, not all teachers will be able to follow through.)

» Requested the recommendation in a way that made the teachers feel important to them.
» When needing a last-minute recommendation (which is more common for scholarships), only asked a teacher who has already completed a similar one in the past.

After each teacher confirmed that they would write a letter of recommendation, my sons responded with a letter that included the following:

1. A "Thank you" for their willingness to assist.
2. A resumé so they would have a general picture of my sons' high school career.
3. A document with a brief description of all their activities, programs, awards, and honors. This gave the recommenders a better context to write with.

This information was also provided to their counselors for their recommendations. This initiative was greatly appreciated because it made it much easier for the recommenders to write their letters.

Organization and planning went a *long* way in making the teachers' and counselors' jobs manageable, thus making it a more pleasant experience to write a recommendation. Here is the strategy we used that was very well received by teachers and counselors:

» Sent a follow-up email to each teacher and counselor who agreed to write a recommendation with a promise to provide a list of requests with dates on an ongoing basis.
» Made the Common App/Coalition App our first request for recommendations in September with a desired deadline of the end of October. We explained that the deadline was to ensure that we could apply Early Decision or Early Action. If known at this time, we included any other requests along with their deadlines.

» Sent a new email every two weeks highlighting any updates and deadlines that were due within a week and thanking them for any recommendations already completed.
» Occasionally, we had to make a request with less than a week to complete it. An email would be sent right away highlighting the request and apologizing for the quick turnaround.

Be sure to send each person their own separate email! Remember that "Please," "Thank You," and "I am sorry" go a long way.

Deadlines—Get organized! Be careful not to be a student that only cares about their own needs and deadlines without respecting the time of others. Teachers and counselors have many students making requests for recommendations so they will be facing a lot of deadlines on top of their normal workload. According to Education Week, "Nationwide, public school counselors are overworked and under-resourced. The average student-to-school-counselor ratio is 482-to-1—nearly double the 250-to-1 ratio recommended by the American School Counselor Association." Nearly a quarter of those students are seniors. At our local school, a teacher will write letters of recommendation for anywhere between 20 and 100 students.

With such a high demand on teachers' and counselors' time, last minute requests can result in rushed and subpar letters of recommendation. Being organized and communicating early and often will greatly assist your teachers and counselors in managing everything on their plate, and this respect of their time may result in a better recommendation for you. Once you have confirmation from each recommender, you should do everything possible to provide a minimum of two weeks' notice for the deadline of your first recommendation. After this point, it is still best to provide a two weeks' notice for subsequent deadlines, with one week being the minimum. You can send a polite reminder one week out and then again two days before.

The consequences of a teacher missing a deadline can be catastrophic. To help prevent this from happening, always provide recommenders with a due date of about three to five days before the actual deadline. If for any reason they miss the deadline you give them, you now have time to request a recommendation from one of the extra teachers on your list. If your counselor misses a deadline, you may have to visit their office to reconcile the problem.

Do NOT ask a teacher every time you see them if the letter of recommendation they have agreed to provide for you has been completed. If you heeded my advice from the Building Relationship section from the junior year chapter, you and your teachers have hopefully been able to get to know each other. So when you see them, unless the deadline is looming, just say hello or simply ask them how they are doing. They know they owe you a recommendation, and your conversation alone will remind them that they need to get it done. Pestering them will only serve as an annoyance and may dissuade them from agreeing to write future recommendations.

Scholarships—Recommendations are important to colleges, and even more so for securing scholarships. Many of the independent scholarship decisions come down to essays and recommendations. Therefore, a glowing recommendation with a strong message goes an awfully long way, so be wise in selecting the person who will write this for you. The choice between using a teacher versus an outside recommender really comes down to who is the better fit for the type of scholarship and who will promote you the best.

The Common and Coalition Apps

Most of the core pieces of your applications were hopefully completed before the end of the summer. If not, you want to complete all of the core, excluding the essay and Activities section, as early in the school year as possible. You should aim to have the Activities, Programs, Awards, & Honors section completed by the end of September.

Once you have confirmation from the teachers you asked to write your letters of recommendation, you may want to wait about one week to enter their details into the application portals. The Common App and Coalition App will send your teachers and counselor an official request and provide them with instructions for uploading their recommendations (which can serve as a reminder). You may notice that each service provides an option for recommendations from other adults, called either "General (Basic) Recommendation" or "Other Recommenders." This option is for anyone who is not a teacher or counselor, such as a coach, employer, pastor, or community leader. Be selective of who you ask to write a general/other recommendation.

Whether it is an optional teacher recommendation or a "general/other" recommender, only include one of these optional recommendations if it provides unique and insightful information or bolsters another part of your application. Be sure that each one of them has something unique to say or just limit yourself to the required number of recommenders. Admissions officers do not want to have their time wasted.

Special Note: Remember to check out websites that provide tips and hints for filling out either of these shared college application portals. Just as I share the lessons we have learned, there is a plethora of sites that offer great guidance for actually filling out the application.

Direct College Applications

Not every school participates in either of the shared application services, so get a jump on any independent college applications now. Most independent applications require very similar information to the common service sites, but some colleges may require significantly more data. When Aaron applied to MIT, it took so much more time than anticipated because we were caught off guard by the vastness of the application process. So do your homework early to be aware of what you are getting yourself in to.

College Essay

College essays matter! You need to engage the person that is taking the time to read your essay.

> *"Your students' college essay is their opportunity to reveal their best qualities and to show an admission committee what makes them stand out from other applicants."* —collegeboard.org

> *"It may sound like a chore, and it will certainly take a substantial amount of work. But it's also a unique opportunity that can make a difference at decision time. Admissions committees put the most weight on your high school grades and your test scores. However, selective colleges receive applications from many worthy students with similar scores and grades—too many to admit. So they use your essay, along with your letters of recommendation and extracurricular activities, to find out what sets you apart from the other talented candidates."* —princetonreview.com

Before starting your essay/personal statement, there are two questions you should answer:

» What do you want the admissions officer to know about you?
» How will your story quickly capture and hold the attention of the reader?

The essay is your chance to tell admissions officers something about who you are and what makes you tick. We all have a story to tell, whether it is our unique background, our exceptional personality, or an interest that is special to us. Admissions officers want to learn about *you* and see if you are a good fit for their school. Make sure not to cross the line between portraying yourself as their ideal candidate and being dishonest about who you really are.

Essay readers do not want to hear you brag about yourself, so do not make the mistake of using your essay to simply rehash accomplishments on your application. You can, however, get away with expounding on an important aspect of your application as long as it used as the basis to tell your story. For example, if you wish to use something listed on your application as the basis of your essay, be sure to talk about why it is so important to you, discuss how it helped shape who you are, and/or explain the difference you want to make as a result of it.

As for writing an engaging or unique essay, one strategy is to incorporate an extended metaphor. The daughter of a good friend, Erica Williams, used this strategy when writing her personal statement and used her love for origami to tell her story. As she described how a simple sheet of paper can produce complex works of art, she illustrated how many aspects of her life that seem simple and independent of each other work together to craft her complex, perfectionistic identity. The content of her essay provided the admissions officer a glimpse into who she was as a person, while the origami metaphor kept the reader engaged and added her personality to the essay.

Without a purposeful message and a theme, it is difficult to write a good college essay. There are many opinions out there on how to craft a great essay. U.S. News has a very good article, "College Essay Examples: How to Write Your Story," which gives good advice and has sample essays (including a different essay that uses origami).

As for timing, you need to develop your ideas for the essay and start formulating your message now. This gives you enough time to actually write the essay, review it, get feedback, and produce your final draft before application deadlines.

START OF OCTOBER

FAFSA & CSS Profile

The portal for FAFSA (Free Application for Federal Student Aid) opens up on **October 1st** for the following school year. Students, you will need to fill out your part before your parent can complete their sections. Do not procrastinate.

> **Parents:** Get ready to divulge all of your personal financial data. FAFSA is the form you need to fill out to get any financial aid from the federal government to help pay for college. It is also used by colleges to determine the amount of any school granted needs-based awards and required by some colleges to give merit scholarships. Unless you plan to pay all college expenses yourself or with private loans, you should fill out FAFSA. It is best to have a complete copy of your previous year's tax forms as you will have to refer to them often. I dealt with merit-based scholarships for all of my boys in three different states, and two of the schools required FAFSA to be filled out every year despite the scholarships not being needs based.

The good thing is that FAFSA is free and can be sent to as many colleges as you need. Make sure you read up on the order you should list colleges on the FAFSA form as this matters in some states. There is a limit of ten schools that you can add to your FAFSA account at one time, but there is a way around this if you plan to apply to eleven or more colleges. Once you confirm that a school on your initial list has received your FAFSA information, you can replace that school with a new one. Just be aware of any conditions, as in some states, it is required to leave in-state schools on the list in a designated order.

In addition to FAFSA, many colleges are now requiring additional forms for financial aid. The most common one is the CSS Profile. The CSS Profile calls for a lot more financial details than FAFSA, which helps colleges get a more complete financial picture of your family. The schools that promise to meet all demonstrated financial need are typically the ones that now require the CSS Profile. While FAFSA is free, the CSS Profile is not. The CSS Profile is run by the College Board, which is the same private company that administers the SAT and the AP program. There is a fee for every college you plan to send the CSS Profile to. Besides the CSS Profile, some colleges have their own additional financial questions while others may use a different service entirely.

You may be required, or have the option, to fill out a state-based financial aid form. Many states have state-sponsored scholarships that are designated for in-state students based on a varying set of criteria. If you plan to take advantage of this type of scholarship, you may be required to fill out the FAFSA form. The idea is to be prepared and get ahead of the game regardless. Know which colleges will require the CSS Profile or an additional form beyond FAFSA (which you should have listed on your College Tracking Spreadsheet).

College Essay

Finish writing your essay during the month of October so that you can:

- » Take time away from the first draft of your essay in order to come back to review it with a fresh perspective.
- » Potentially submit an application through a school's Early Action or Early Decision program (most of these due dates are October 31 or November 1).
- » Have your essay reviewed by someone who is capable of reading it objectively (preferably someone who does not know you that well personally) in order to get an unbiased opinion of it. Ask

Before The Application

> this person to tell you what they learned about you and how engaging they found the story.
> » Request for someone that does know you well to tell you what they gained from the essay and whether they believe it represents a true reflection of you. Also ask this person if they found the story engaging.

Once you have the right story and the right message, PLEASE, PLEASE, PLEASE review your essay for errors in grammar and spelling. Then have someone else review the essay who is capable of finding any remaining grammatical errors or punctuation mistakes. Then, have another person review your essay for clarity and to find any remaining errors. You want to get reviewers who will provide honest feedback. You can use one of your teachers or a fellow student that you know is a great writer. Submitting an essay with errors will definitely be a strike against you.

THANKSGIVING BREAK

Evaluation Time

It is time to evaluate your college application progress. Here are two items you want to ensure are complete during your break regarding your tracking spreadsheet.

1. The choices in your College Pool have been pared down to the schools you will apply to.
2. Each college has every detail filled out in the spreadsheet.

At this stage of the application season, there should be no surprises or unknowns. You must understand all the application requirements you are facing and their associated deadlines. Put all of your deadlines into a calendar, and then set reminders for a week in advance of every deadline. Double-check every deadline to make sure you did not record them incorrectly and to confirm that none of the deadlines have changed.

It is very important to monitor counselor and teacher recommendation deadlines. It is best to provide them with a deadline of at least a week before it is truly due. This provides enough time to find someone else if a recommender will not be able to follow through with their commitment. Be aware that the shared application services list deadlines for the colleges you select, and the counselors can see these dates. This is why it is important to provide them with your preferred deadline, especially if you are attempting to meet a scholarship deadline not reflected by the default date.

Scholarships

Continue to do research for potential scholarships and update your scholarship tracking spreadsheet. Regularly review the spreadsheet for any upcoming deadlines and set reminders on your calendar for these as well.

> **Parents**: Your kids will have a lot on their plate during this season. Assisting with deadline reminders is a great way to help them stay organized. However, be cautious that your assistance does not add to their stress levels.

Application

Ideally, most parts of your college applications should be completed by this point, except for possibly the essay. For any schools with early to mid-December deadlines, the entire application needs to be completed by the end of this break, especially if you are going to be competing for scholarships. This does not mean you must submit the application by the end of the Thanksgiving break; you just want ample time to walk away and come back later to review it with a fresh set of eyes. Anything completed at the last moment, or reviewed just before submitting it, is prone to have errors and mistakes that are easy to overlook. Precision is key because you do not ever want to give anyone an excuse to associate anything negative with your work.

Even if you have deadlines that are in late December or January, there are benefits to completing the application during your Thanksgiving break. After this break comes the push to the end of the semester, which means papers, reports, projects, and studying for finals. Completing your applications now will help you avoid a great deal of stress. Moreover, submitting an application well before a deadline has advantages for several reasons:

- » Application reviewers are excited for the new crop of applicants.
- » Application reviewers are not overwhelmed or worn out yet.
- » It appears that you prioritized applying to their college, which sends the message that you are serious about their school.

Christmas Break

Continue working through your college and scholarship tracking spreadsheets and stay on top of your deadlines. Then get some well-earned rest and relaxation. You have been working hard and you deserve some downtime. Sit back and appreciate all the work you put in over the summer to stay ahead in this crazy application process. Refresh for the final semester of high school. With the application process soon to be a thing of the past, get ready to enjoy the relief of knowing you did everything to the best of your ability. Granted, you must stay focused on your schoolwork for the next four months or so because you do not want all your previous hard work to be undone.

Julia Says

You should be done with college applications by the second semester, so I highly recommend that you prioritize enjoying the time you have left in high school. This is the best time for you to mentally enjoy yourself; hang out with friends, attend prom, and go to senior festivities. Make memories and enjoy yourself! As far as schoolwork goes, you should still make sure to maintain your grades and apply to scholarships. Once you get into a college, they will want to see your transcript from both semesters of this year. Other than that, take a breather, you earned it. You have been working towards this moment for 18 years! From here, you will be starting a new educational journey in college, so please take advantage of the time you will have during the second semester and the upcoming summer!

Transcript

As soon as grades are released from your first semester, have your counselor send a mid-year report to all the schools you have already applied to. For every college you applied to using an application portal, be sure to use that same system to send the mid-year report **and** notify your counselor to submit the report to that portal.

APRIL

Admissions Notifications

You should receive the vast majority of your college admissions decisions by the beginning of April. I will let you in on a little secret—most students do not get into all of the schools they apply to, including the ones they had their hearts set on for years. It is not a knock on you in any way. Colleges have more candidates than they have room to admit, and probably over 90% of those applying are qualified. Colleges do not simply take the highest ranked applicants and accept them.

Many external factors go into selecting their pool of acceptances:

» **Demographics**—Most colleges want students from all over the country and world, a mix of urban and rural areas, and a range of economic statuses. Colleges also need money to function, which means they require some wealthy families that can pay 100% of the school's costs and hopefully become future donors.

» **Diversity**—If everyone brings the same perspective to a conversation in any setting, how will anyone learn or grow? Diversity of thought exposes us to the viewpoints of people that do not think or act like us. Diversity on a college campus helps prepare you to go anywhere in the world and respect others who are different from you. Without diversity, you will be limited in your growth as a person.

» **Roles**—Many selective colleges need to fill roles and seek students who are the best at what they do. If a school needs a first chair trombone player this upcoming year and you are great on clarinet, you may miss out on that school. Yet, if you are a decorated debater and the college is looking to start a debate team, this may just be the lucky break you need to get in over applicants with otherwise stronger applications.

» **Fit**—Not every college is a good fit for every student. For example, a teacher recommendation could explain that a student's test anxiety affected their grades despite being the brightest in their class. This clarification may help with most colleges, but a super competitive school may not accept this student based on research that says students with test anxiety do not fare well at their university.

» **Gaps**—Certain professional fields have gaps in the marketplace that colleges want to help fill. For example, the low number of women in technology has been a gap for way too long and colleges are purposefully working to address this disparity.

I hope and pray you get into every college you apply to. As amazing as my kids were in high school (yes, I am biased), they had their share of rejections. A "no" in our household was viewed merely as a step towards narrowing down our list of choices. Yes, it may be a bit disappointing, but you cannot attend every college that accepts you anyway. If you took the proper approach of only applying to colleges you are willing to attend, you really only need one acceptance. I will say that my kids' acceptance rates and scholarship offers were decidedly higher than most students in our community, and their success as strong candidates was due to the information I am sharing with you now.

College Decision

Do your homework—During the month of April, you must evaluate your options in order to make an informed college choice before "Decision Day" (typically May 1st). Every student has their own set of criteria for what is most important when making this decision. Whatever your criteria, the trick is to separate myth from reality. The information advertised by each college will gloss over most negative aspects of the school. Dig a little deeper before making your final decision. You will surely hear negative comments about any school, so you must always consider the source and the magnitude of complaints. Aaron was aware when he committed to his college that their dining services did not have a great reputation, but he determined that this was just not that important to him. At the same time, Christopher turned down a full scholarship to a school that ranked highest amongst his options for his intended major because the culture was a bad fit for him.

Before The Application

Be sure to visit—If you have not visited each of the schools that made your final list, try your best to do so in April before making a final decision. Some schools may even fly you in for a visit, especially if they have offered you a scholarship. Until you step on campus to get a feel for it yourself, I believe you are making an uninformed decision. If you do make the trip, arrange an appointment to visit the offices of your intended major and any programs you may get involved with.

Do full comparisons—Do not pick a school based on reputation or scholarship only; consider the entire package. Getting a free education should not come with a high personal cost such as attending a school that does not offer your major or an environment where you will be miserable. Similarly, going to a very prestigious school may not pay off if your acquired debt is too high when you graduate. My oldest graduated from the University of Kentucky, and we are very grateful for the opportunity they provided for him. As he was deciding between law schools, he attended an open house at Georgetown Law for admitted students. They covered the financial requirements where the estimated cost over three years was over a quarter of a million dollars. Students from Ivy League schools and other top private institutions were already saddled with that kind of debt. It was in that moment that Christopher fully realized the advantage he had by choosing the best overall package for undergraduate college instead of choosing a prestigious college and taking on student loans.

College choice calculator—I created a College Choice Calculator Spreadsheet* to assist my boys with making their final decision. Students can use it to consider the different aspects of selecting a college, rate how important each factor is to them, and then self-assess colleges based on how well they perform in each category. I have used this process with several other students, and they all appreciated the methodical approach.

* *This spreadsheet can be purchased at woolfolkworks.com/templates.*

Special programs—If you plan to participate in a non-traditional program at your future college, gather all the facts about the program. This is especially true for programs that take place abroad. Special program expenses vary from college to college, and they can get quite pricey. Do not assume that most of the costs will be covered by your tuition. Consider costs like travel, visas, and required spending money. If you cannot get straightforward answers to these questions, reach out to students who have already participated in the program. Do not take a school representative's spoken words as fact. Get the details in writing.

Post Decision Day offers—Once Decision Day has passed, colleges will have an accurate picture of their scholarship pools. It is possible to hear from a college you have already been accepted to with an upgrade to their financial package offering. Granted, you likely will have already accepted an offer and paid a deposit to another school, so you will have to part with your deposit if the new offer is better. Before officially cancelling an offer from a college, ensure you know whether your acceptance is binding. For example, Early Decision acceptances are typically financially binding.

Planned transfer—A planned transfer is when you start at one institution with a clear intention to transfer to another institution to finish your college degree. Here are two reasons to consider starting your college career in anticipation of a planned transfer:

1. The school you want to attend is not affordable for all four years.
2. You did not get into your dream school initially.

If you are not able to attend a college you have been accepted to due to financial reasons, contact the school and discuss a future transfer as an option. Many expensive schools will suggest taking courses at another college for two years at a lower cost, and then transferring over to their school to finish your degree. Be sure to coordinate the schools and the specific courses to ensure a smooth transition.

If you did not get accepted to your dream school, your first step is to contact the school and ask from which colleges are students the most successful in transferring. Transfer acceptance rates do not follow the same levels as first-time acceptance rates. The normal acceptance rates for Harvard and Princeton are around 5-6% and their transfer acceptance rates are below 1%. Yet, Washington University in St. Louis has a 20% transfer acceptance rate and Vanderbilt's is 25%, both significantly higher than their regular acceptance rates.

If you decide to go the transfer route, you must be absolutely focused on being a high-level learner committed to excellence from the very beginning of your freshman year because you will need to demonstrate a high level of success on you transfer application.

Decline offers officially—As your offers start to roll in, you will begin to narrow down your list of colleges to choose between. Once you know for sure that you will not attend a certain college, the polite thing to do is inform them of your decision. There are students on the wait list that will appreciate your kindness, especially if you are declining an acceptance that includes a scholarship. This may free up funds that will give an opportunity for another student to attend that college.

Be prepared to answer a short survey regarding why you made your decision to turn down their offer. These surveys only take a few minutes and will help the next set of students about to go through the college application process. On the positive side, declining offers will stop unwanted calls and emails. The drawback is that on the slight chance they have additional funds after Decision Day, they may not contact you with a better offer.

Negotiation—I believe that everything in life can be negotiated, even when the probability of success is miniscule. Most colleges are simply not willing to negotiate... but what if they are? Our family was not successful in our attempts to negotiate, but I know other students who were triumphant. If two schools of equal stature have offered you a scholarship, try pitting one school against the other. If you have a better offer to an equally or higher ranked school than the one you prefer to attend, see if they are willing to match or improve their offer. *Road 2 College* offers advice in their article, "How Do You Negotiate College Tuition? 5 Tips to Getting a Better Deal from Your College."

If you decide to negotiate, please take heed of this advice:

» Do ***not*** lie!
» Do not bother to negotiate a deal if you are not willing to accept an offer on the spot if they agree to your terms.
» Avoid including conditions or ultimatums (but if you plan to, be *absolutely sure* you are prepared to follow through).

Thus far, I have only seen negotiations work with private colleges. Chances for success may not be great, but you cannot win if you do not play.

MAY

Excitement Phase

Before high school lets out, you will be in your excitement phase. Experiencing the anticipation of graduation along with the eagerness to attend your new college is a great feeling. Enjoy the moment, it is your time to shine! You worked hard to get where you are. In the midst of your elatedness, do not forget to thank all the people who helped you reach this point. It truly takes a village to raise a child, so let the teachers, mentors, counselors, relatives, coaches, and friends that supported you along the way celebrate with you.

You are now at the point where you have made your college choice. You may be attending a dream or stretch school, or maybe a target or safe school. Your new focus should now be on your "next": your

Before The Application

intended career. You are now on *your* path and there is no looking back. You have made the best decision available to you—no regrets and no takebacks. Just as in all aspects of life, you must take full advantage of the opportunities offered to you. My wife, Dedra, attended undergrad at Morris Brown College, a small HBCU (Historically Black College or University). Six years later, she obtained her PhD in Pharmacology from Emory University along with peers that went to some of our nation's top universities. I already mentioned how my eldest son attended the University of Kentucky and went on to be accepted to four of the top-twenty ranked law schools in the country (and was waitlisted to another two, including Harvard). I share our stories to encourage you to move forward with a plan to success. Remember: whatever the destination, there is no single path to get there.

College Check List

» **Blogs**—Join blogs and social media groups with your future classmates. You may end up making friends before you even move in.
» **Orientation**—At most schools, orientations are mandatory and take place in the summer. Your family needs to review the available date options and sign up right away because they fill up fast. Housing for orientation is usually covered for students but rarely for parents.
» **Housing**—Most colleges require freshmen to stay on campus. Research the housing selection website and make sure you know how the process works and when it takes place. Be ready to register the minute your time slot opens because room availability dwindles very quickly. Have multiple options to choose from because your first choice will not always be available. No matter where you end up living, make the best of it and have fun.
» **Meal plan**—Many colleges require freshmen to select a meal

plan. Determine what fits your budget and know that many freshmen do not eat at dining halls as often as they thought they would. Review the school's policy for upgrading or downgrading meal plans. Downgrading a meal plan is rarely allowed, but upgrading is usually offered, so it may be strategic to start with a cheaper plan and upgrade later if necessary.

» **Roommates**—Finding a good roommate is not an exact science. All three of my boys left it to chance their freshman year and it worked out well for each of them. At the same time, I have heard nightmare stories regarding roommates. You know if you can get along with anybody or if you need to avoid certain types of people, so let this determine whether you search for a roommate or leave it to chance. Heed this warning: **many good friendships have been destroyed by becoming college roommates.** Consider this before choosing to live with your best friend from high school.

END OF SCHOOL YEAR

Transcript

Before school lets out, let your counselor know which school you will be attending and request that an official copy of your transcript be sent to your college. This request should be made through whichever platform you used to apply to the college. Be aware that if you apply through the Common App, your counselor can only send the report once, so be sure you have made your final decision before making your request. Also, get an official version of your transcript for your personal use.

Post-Graduation—Starting College Strong

You must be purposeful to be successful in college!

"There is no secret to success. It is the result of preparation, hard work, and learning from failure."
–General Colin Powell

Every ending should be the start of a new beginning, and every beginning can influence how and if you achieve your next ending. Just as you planned in high school for your "next," start your college career with your "next" in mind.

In this chapter, I will share a bit of wisdom as you prepare for the next major transition in your life. My objective is to:

- » Encourage you to become a **lifelong learner**
- » Show you the importance of doing a **reset** from the celebratory state of graduation to a preparatory state to begin college
- » Walk you through a comparison of high school versus college grading
- » Explain why your college GPA will also be important when you graduate
- » Encourage you to build a plan for college success
- » Urge you to continue to search for scholarships, even after you have started college

Before The Application

» Discuss the pros and cons of applying all of your eligible college credits
» Advise you to conduct a bit more research to learn more about your new school and its surroundings

Pre-College Focus Point: During freshman orientation at the Air Force Academy, we were instructed to look at the cadet to our left and then look at the cadet to our right, because one among the three of us would not be there in four years for graduation. This was once a common practice at many college orientations.

> *"The official four-year graduation rate for students attending public colleges and universities is 33.3%. The six-year rate is 57.6%. At private colleges and universities, the four-year graduation rate is 52.8%, and 65.4% earn a degree in six years."*
> *–College Insider with Lynn O'Shaughnessy*

These numbers, as reported by the federal government, are staggering. *Extending graduation beyond four years makes college an awfully expensive investment.* Not graduating from college at all represents a major investment in time and money with no return. In this book, I made it a point to cover the importance of ***discipline*** as it relates to your success at the next level. Lack of discipline in your actions and an inability to remain organized will almost certainly guarantee that you will struggle in college.

One of the best lessons I have learned from my minister, Walter S. Poole, Sr. (Ben Hill Christian Church in SW Atlanta), is to "know why you do what you do." You are going to college for the purpose of gaining a marketable skillset in order to secure gainful employment in a field of your choosing. Along the way you will meet new friends, make a lot of great memories, and evolve from a dependent kid into an independent adult. College will impart many great lessons outside of the classroom. You should explore new activities in search for experiences beyond what you have faced so far in life. Brian and Aaron decided to try intramural soccer, Brian played coed volleyball despite having never really played before, and Christopher tried flag football for the first time ever. Brian made my wife quite nervous when he called home to ask if we would pay for him to take a boxing class. I still laugh about the time he said he "forgot to duck."

The college experience should be much more than just schoolwork. You need stress outlets to maintain your sanity. However, you will have problems if you do not maintain a balance. The power of the word "NO" must be used in college. This chapter will give you several valuable tips to focus on as you prepare to transition to college.

Love Being a Learner

Most students cannot wait for their current stage of school to be over. Eighth graders count down the days until the end of middle school. Seniors in high school cannot wait to graduate and move on to the next phase of their lives. College seniors anticipate the day school is over, excited with the idea of never entering another classroom ever again. These feelings are understandable after being in school for so long, but school and learning are not one and the same. Life should be a continuous journey of education so that our minds continue to grow.

Every day, the world changes and advances. The knowledge and skillsets people obtained fifteen years ago must be adapted to today's world. The knowledge you obtain today will have to adapt in order to still be relevant in 15 years. Students that graduated high school ten to fifteen years ago grew up developing the skill to find information from encyclopedias. Imagine how out of date these people would be in the modern world if they had not adapted their skillset to find credible information via the internet. In life, those who choose to stop learning or stop growing eventually get left behind, and too often their opinions are formed by others who tell them what to think. One day, school will truly be over for you, but never allow the desire for knowledge to wane away... and NEVER stop reading!

Post-Graduation Essentials— Taking it Forward

Julia Says

As you are just months away from starting a new academic journey, I want to leave you with some words of encouragement and wisdom. Use this time to take a mental reset. Let your mind and your body take a breather. You have been working for four years straight through all-nighters, internships, clubs, volunteer work, and everything else under the sun. Now you need to take the time to rejuvenate yourself before jumping into another academic cycle that may be even more intense than what you endured in high school.

This summer, do things that you enjoy and bring you mental peace. Whether it is hanging with your friends at the pool or finishing that book collecting dust on your shelf, the activities you choose should help refresh your body and mind of any and all stress from the past four years. At this point, I hope that you know what your mind needs so that you can fully utilize this summer to mentally prepare yourself for college. Even if you do not have yourself figured out, there is no better time than the present to start. Do not make the mistake of thinking that it is too late to achieve certain goals as I did. Discover yourself, get your education, and dream big. You are still young, so take advantage of every second of it. You are capable of more than you know.

Reset

Graduation is over, the parties are in the past, and graduation gifts are now in hand. It is time to reset after one of the best chapters in your life. Every ending should be the foundation for a new beginning. The past is just that, so keep it in its proper place. Learn from the past but do not live in it. If you rely on the great things you did back in high school, the rest of the world will catch up and pass you by. If you stew in the troubles of the past, you will not be able to unveil your wonderful, undiscovered talents. Therefore, it is best to live in the present while at the same time planning for a bright, but unknown, future. Make sure that focusing on your ambitions does not interfere with a healthy appreciation for the simple things in life. This is a delicate balance, I know.

A reset is taking inventory of where you are and recognizing what you need to move forward. Let us start the reset:

- » **Be purposeful**—It does not matter what college you attend if you do not end up with a degree. Go into college with a purpose along with a plan to be successful.
- » **Make the transition**—In high school, you may have performed for good grades by memorizing topics for tests and mimicking skills to earn grades, all without actually learning the material. This approach does not fare well in college. Make sure to complete transition from being a *performer* to becoming a *learner*. The mere ability to recite material will not be sufficient for success in a college classroom. You must be able to competently apply the knowledge you have been taught in order to demonstrate your full understanding of the concepts. This means you must learn both the "how" and the "why" of the material.
- » **Starting strong**—Take advantage of your first year of college. Even though classes will be taught in more detail and at a faster pace, you have been already exposed to the content of some core college courses during college prep classes in high school.

Use this to your advantage. It is much easier to maintain a good GPA throughout college if it starts high your freshman year. However, do not overwhelm yourself during the first few months of college. Ease into any extracurriculars and your social life while you adjust to a different lifestyle and the new rigors of school.

» **Relationships matter**—You do not just take a class, but you take a professor of a certain subject. Get to know your professor when you can. Becoming familiar with your professor helps you understand their style of teaching and how they wish for you to demonstrate your knowledge on a test. ***Go to your professor's office hours***. My wife, Dr. Woolfolk, has been a college professor for over fifteen years and she rarely gets visits from the very students that struggle in her class and complain about their grade at the end of the year. Inevitably, professors share more in one-on-one conversations and will sometimes unintentionally share some useful tips or hints.

» **Finding your niche** –The cool thing about college is that you will no longer have to be like an elephant that is judged by its ability to climb a tree.

Fair Selection. [Unknown digital image]. (n.d.). Retrieved from: Google search. *http://scholasticadministrator.typepad.com/thisweekineducation/2012/08/ cartoons-climb-that-tree.html#.WiJU90pKtPY*

High schools use a cookie-cutter approach to teaching and reward students who are able to "perform" well in *all* subjects. This leaves students who have a specialized skill set feeling inadequate. College allows you to find your niche and home in on your specialty. Embrace the idea that we all have different strengths and that you now have the opportunity to develop yours.

Courage—One of the biggest dream killers in life is submitting to fear. Striving for success will create doubts and fears, especially when you dream big. Courage is not the replacement of fear, but the mindset required to overcome fear. I want you to have the courage to go big! You will have moments of doubt where you will wonder if you are good or smart enough, especially when the people around you will seem to have it all together while you do not. While this is not the most comfortable place to be, it does mean that you are challenging and pushing yourself towards greatness. In these moments, use your courage to persevere.

Post-Graduation Timeline—Next Level Planning

SUMMER BEFORE COLLEGE

Grade Review

Your final grade for a class in high school is typically comprised of tests, quizzes, homework, papers, in-class assignments, class participation, extra-credit, etc. After graduating from high school, I had each of my kids calculate a new final grade for their last two or three semesters based only on their scores for tests, quizzes, research papers, reports, and essays. We then compared the grade they actually achieved in each class to this new calculation.

Before The Application

Example of an actual transcript (extra credit included in scores):

Class	Score	Weight	Weighted Score
Final	90	15%	13.5
Midterm	86	10%	8.6
Tests	85	20%	17
Paper/Essay/Report	90	10%	9
Homework	100	15%	15
Quizzes	95	15%	14.2
In-Class Assignments	98	10%	9.8
Class Participation	100	5%	5
Total Points		**100%**	**92.2**

Example of recalculating transcript (extra credit removed from scores):

Class	Score	Weight	Weighted Score
Final	88	25%	22
Midterm	85	15%	12.7
Tests	83	25%	20.7
Paper/Essay/Report	90	15%	13.5
Quizzes	95	20%	19
Total Points		**100%**	**87.9**

This points towards the reality of grading in college versus high school. You will still have classes with in-class assignments, homework assignments, and class participation requirements, but in high school these were often designed to boost your scores along with extra credit. This will typically no longer be the case. Your final grades in college will be largely decided by fewer assignments, which makes it more difficult to recover, and these assignments will require much more effort. For example, since a great deal of your learning comes from doing work outside of the classroom, homework is much more intensive.

Doing this exercise with my boys was a real eye-opener for the need to improve their study habits and learning ability. I hope this encourages you, as a rising college student, to build a plan to address the new demands of the college classroom.

Your College GPA Matters

I have continuously stressed how important your high school GPA is for your "next." The same will hold true for your college GPA. Just as your high school GPA mattered for getting into college, your college GPA will help you reach your "next," which could be graduate school, professional school, or your first job. If you plan to continue your education after earning your undergraduate degree, be prepared to go through a similar process as what you just had with college admissions. If you plan to enter the workforce immediately after college, hiring managers will look at your GPA as an indicator for work success in the same way that admissions officers use it as an indicator of success for their school.

I have given you many tips to help you prepare for success in college, and I strongly suggest that you build a plan to properly navigate college the same way you did for high school. It is much easier to maintain a strong GPA when you start strong. Starting strong in college requires discipline, and for most teens, being disciplined requires a plan!

Building a College Plan

I was not ready for the challenges of college when I graduated high school because I was too accustomed to being a performer. I pretended

Before The Application

to be the ideal high school student without considering what it would take to be successful at the college level. I did not know how to learn because I spent my high school years studying to get a certain grade, and I was able to use homework and in-class assignments to compensate for when I did poorly on papers that I neglected. So, I had no idea how to organize my work or manage my time when I got to college.

As a father, I was determined to make sure my children would not struggle the way I did. When Christopher was preparing to head off to college, I did an in-depth search for resources that would help him with this transition. It turns out that the very first website (**howtostudyincollege.com**) I found back then is still the best resource I have come across to date. I truly wish I had the insights from this website when I went off to college.

I have recommended *howtostudyincollege.com* to every college student I know. The lessons shared on this website have served our family extremely well for over seven years with great results. The key information provided on this website has always been free. I do not know the owner and I receive no compensation from recommending his site. This site has grown and improved since we discovered it in 2013, and it now offers an app that pairs with his program.

Scholarships

Many students are not aware of the number of scholarships available to students already enrolled in college. Do not give up on bringing down your out-of-pocket expenses for college. Just as you did in high school, create a Scholarship Tracking spreadsheet to use throughout college. Look for scholarships geared towards your major or area of discipline. Some colleges offer departmental scholarships to students who perform well in college, especially to those who get involved through activities like research.

Class Registration

Time Slots—A lot of freshmen will be vying for the same classes during the first two semesters of college. This makes planning for class registration important, especially at medium and larger colleges.

Advisement—Most schools will require you to speak to an academic advisor before registering for classes. These may be professors in the department of your major who have busy schedules. Most advisors are very informative, but they may not always provide the best information for your unique goals. You should go into the meeting with a plan and use your advisor for guidance. Explore ahead of time to understand the required courses for your major and college along with the order they need to be taken. If you are not certain about your major, focus more on the core requirements during your freshman year.

Time of day—When planning for your first-choice time slots, figure out if you are truly a morning person before scheduling any 8:00 AM classes. My number one rule for college students is to ***never*** miss a class. This rule is often broken when students opt for early morning classes. On the other hand, late afternoon or evening classes may conflict with any organizational meetings or intramural sports you wish to participate in.

Registration planning—There may not always be available seats for classes in your preferred time slots. *Go into registration with alternative options for time slots and courses.* Find out from the registrar's office ahead of time what happens if a required course runs out of seats. Then, ask upperclassmen how they handle full classes. Typically, there is a lot of jostling of schedules during and after the registration period that may free up available slots.

College Credits—Dual enrollment, AP exams, and IB exams provide great opportunities for receiving college credit. If you performed well enough to earn credits, take a minute to review the pros and cons of applying them.

Pros of taking the credit:
- » May allow you to graduate sooner, therefore saving money.
- » May allow you to explore more elective classes you may be interested in.
- » May allow you to pursue a dual major.
- » May allow you to choose an atypical minor or even two minors.

Pros of not taking the credit:
- » May help you obtain a stronger grasp of the material.
- » May help you learn the material in the way the college likes to teach it.
- » May help you build confidence in college.
- » May help you establish a strong GPA (useful for scholarships).

The bottom line is to "know thyself" and not put yourself in a position to fail, while taking full advantage of whichever option places you in the best position for success.

Deeper Research

You will learn a lot about your college at orientation. While there, take the time to ask about the "other stuff" you will want to know when you arrive on campus. If you do not get answers at orientation, you can search for answers over the summer or ask on a blog. Here are some examples of questions you may want to find the answers to:

- » Where are some good places to eat around campus or in the surrounding area?
- » Where are the best places to shop for groceries and personal items?

Post-Graduation—Starting College Strong

» Where are the best places to go for hair appointments?
» Where is a good and reasonable mechanic (if bringing a car)?
» Where is the best place to go for a medical emergency?
» What are the best ways to score tickets to big games?
» What are some essentials for a dorm room?
» Is there a writing center?
» Are there any professors to avoid?
» Are there any areas of town that should be avoided?

My Farewell

My Hope for You

I hope that you were able to take full advantage of the model I provided and built your sturdy wheels and quality car to drive off to college. I hope that you were able to secure an ideal college that is a great fit for you. I hope that one day soon you will be able to secure your ideal career. Finally, I hope that you are able to live out the life of your dreams for many years to come.

My Words of Wisdom

I desire to share with you a few of words of wisdom gained through the experience of life. College, career, and wealth may possibly make you happy, but that happiness only lasts for a while. Therefore, I want to encourage you to find long-lasting happiness… or even better than that, JOY! True happiness can be found through:

- » Building meaningful relationships
- » Fulfilling your passion—whether as part of your career or not
- » Discovering your purpose in life
- » Making a difference in your community
- » Helping someone else achieve their dreams
- » Finding the balance between chasing after or achieving life goals (internal) and having true happiness (external).

Before The Application

My Source of Joy

The greatest source of happiness in my life comes from family. Number one is my awesome wife Dedra followed by my three amazing children. I also have a very close-knit extended family that I greatly depend on as well, especially my mother, Barbara J. Woolfolk. Yet, the most important influence in my life comes from the true source of my joy, which is my Father in Heaven and my personal savior, Jesus.

I leave you with more than my hope, and that is my prayer that you find your balance in life with both ***happiness*** and ***joy***.

My Personal Reward

I worked for 29 years in the tech field and truly enjoyed each role along the way. While actively pursuing my career goals, I found my purpose while working with teens to share knowledge and wisdom, open up new opportunities, and provide hope. The reward of watching a young person succeed in what they have planned for themselves completely outweighs my own personal accomplishments. I would love to hear your stories. Please share them at my website, *woolfolkworks.com/mystory*.

Notes

Before We Get Started—Our Story
Maldonado, Camilo. "Price Of College Increasing Almost 8 Times Faster Than Wages." Forbes, 25 July 2018, *www.forbes.com/sites/camilomaldonado/2018/07/24/price-of-college-increasing-almost-8-times-faster-than-wages/#2b9f145066c1*.

Friedman, Zack. "Student Loan Debt Statistics In 2020: A Record $1.6 Trillion." Forbes, 5 Feb. 2020, *www.forbes.com/sites/zackfriedman/2020/02/03/student-loan-debt-statistics/#54818589281f*.

Planning For Success—The Plan
Mulhere, Kaitlin. "These 75 Colleges Promise to Meet 100% of Students' Financial Need." Yahoo Money, 12 Nov. 2019, *www.yahoo.com/amphtml/money/75-colleges-promise-meet-100-161539583.html*.

Ninth Grade—The Fundamentals—Reading For Fun
Sullivan, Patrick. "An Open Letter to High School Students about Reading." Ponte Vedra High School, *www-pvhs.stjohns.k12.fl.us/wp-content/uploads/2017/04/OpenLetter.pdf*. Accessed 24 Aug. 2020.

Ehmke, Rachel. "How Using Social Media Affects Teenagers." Child Mind Institute, *childmind.org/article/how-using-social-media-affects-teenagers*. Accessed 24 Aug. 2020.

Hilliard, Jena. "What Is Social Media Addiction." Addiction Center, 18 June 2020, *www.addictioncenter.com/drugs/social-media-addiction*.

Ninth Grade Timeline—Spring Break—College Majors
Data Point. "Beginning College Students Who Change Their Majors Within 3 Years of Enrollment." National Center for Education Statistics, U.S. Department of Education, Dec. 2017, *nces.ed.gov/datapoints/2018434.asp#:%7E:text=About%20one%2Dthird%20of%20students,percent%20of%20bachelor's%20degree%20students.*

Ninth Grade Timeline—Summer Break—ACT/SAT Focus
"About the PSAT Test." The Princeton Review, TPR Education IP Holdings, LLC, *www.princetonreview.com/college/psat-information*. Accessed 24 Aug. 2020.

Ninth Grade Timeline—Summer Break—Discipline—Focus on Organization
Lesco, Patrick. "Why Is It Important to Be Organized in College?" The Classroom, Leaf Group Ltd., *www.theclassroom.com/important-organized-college-6323892.html*. Accessed 24 Aug. 2020.

Logsdon, Ann. "How Planners Help Students Learn Organizational Skills." Verywell Family, About, Inc. (Dotdash), 31 Jan. 2020, *www.verywellfamily.com/teach-planning-and-organizational-skills-2162269*.

Tenth Grade—The Fundamentals—Reading For Fun
Heisler, Kayla. "Here's How Many Books the Average CEO Reads Yearly — And What They're Reading." Fairygodboss, 11 May 2018, *fairygodboss.com/articles/here-s-how-many-books-the-average-ceo-reads-yearly#:%7E:text=In%20fact%2C%20the%20average%20number,ability%20to%20reach%20higher%20ground.%E2%80%9D*.

Tenth Grade—Sophomore Secrets—The Accountability Transition
"7 Reasons—Other than Cost—That Students Don't Graduate." EAB, 15 Apr. 2019, *eab.com/insights/daily-briefing/student-success/7-reasons-other-than-cost-that-students-dont-graduate*.

Tenth Grade Timeline—Spring Break—College Tracking Spreadsheet
Berkman, J. (2018, July 27). How Many Colleges Should You Apply To? *PrepScholar*. *https://blog.prepscholar.com/how-many-colleges-should-i-apply-to*

IvyWise. (2020, April 29). Your Balanced College List: How Many Colleges You Should Apply To? *https://www.ivywise.com/ivywise-knowledgebase/resources/article/ your-balanced-college-list-how-many-colleges-you-should-apply-to/#:%7E:text=At%20 IvyWise%2C%20we%20advise%20that,they%20were%20accepted%20 early%20decision.*

Edmonds, D. (2015, November 20). How Many College Applications Are Too Many? Forbes. *https://www.forbes.com/sites/noodleeducation/2015/11/20/how-many-olleges-should-you-apply-to/#70949ae549ef*

How Do You Negotiate College Tuition? 5 Tips to Getting a Better Deal From Your College. (2020, September 29). Road 2 College. *https://www.road2college.com/ how-do-you-negotiate-college-tuition/*

Eleventh Grade—The Fundamentals—ACT/SAT Prep
Muniz, H. (2020, August 16). ACT vs SAT: 11 Key Differences to Help You Pick the Right Test. *PrepScholar. https://blog.prepscholar.com/act-vs-sat*

The College Application—Activities / Programs / Awards / Honors Descriptions
Perkins, Jon. "15 Mistakes to Avoid on the Common App 'Activities' Section." Essaywise, 9 Oct. 2015, *www.essaywise.com/blogposts/15-mistakes-to-avoid-on-the-common-app-activities-section.*

The College Application—College Essay
Sawyer, Ethan. "12 Great Personal Statement Examples For College Applications." College Essay Guy, *www.collegeessayguy.com/blog/personal-statement-examples-for-college.* Accessed 24 Aug. 2020.

The College Application—College Interviews
Berkman, Justin. "The 14 College Interview Questions You Must Prepare For." PrepScholar, 27 Jan. 2020, *blog.prepscholar.com/college-interview-questions-you-should-prepare-for.*

The College Application—Social Media Footprint
15 Things Colleges Will Look for in Your Social Media Accounts. (n.d.). Veritas Prep. Retrieved September 22, 2020, from *https://www.veritasprep.com/college/ college-admissions-social-media-strategy/*

Senior Timeline—By End of September—Letters of Recommendation
Fuschillo, Alanna. "The Troubling Student-to-Counselor Ratio That Doesn't Add Up." Education Week, Editorial Projects in Education, 14 Aug. 2018, *www.edweek.org/ew/articles/2018/08/14/the-troubling-student-to-counselor-ratio-that-doesnt-add.html#:%7E:text=The%20average%20student%2Dto%2Dschool,the%20American%20School%20Counselor%20Association.*

Senior Timeline—By End of September—College Essay
College Application Essay. (n.d.). College Board. Retrieved September 15, 2020, from *https://professionals.collegeboard.org/guidance/applications/essay*

Senior Timeline—By End of September—College Essay
The Princeton Review. (n.d.). Crafting an Unforgettable College Essay. TPR Education IP Holdings. Retrieved September 15, 2020, from *https://www.princetonreview.com/college-advice/college-essay*

Senior Timeline—By End of September—College Essay
Moody, Josh. "College Essay Examples: How to Write Your Story." US News and World Report, 24 Apr. 2019, *www.usnews.com/education/best-colleges/articles/2019-04-24/college-essay-examples-how-to-write-your-story.*

Senior Timeline—April—College Decision
How Do You Negotiate College Tuition? 5 Tips to Getting a Better Deal From Your College. (2020, September 29). Road 2 College. *https://www.road2college.com/how-do-you-negotiate-college-tuition/*

Pre College—Pre-College Focus Point
O'Shaughnessy, Lynn. "Federal Government Publishes More Complete Graduation Rate Data." Cappex.Com, *www.cappex.com/articles/blog/government-publishes-graduation-rate-data#:%7E:text=The%20official%20four%2Dyear%20graduation,%2Dyear%20rate%20is%2057.6%25. Accessed 24 Aug. 2020.*

Index

A
Accountability transition 86
    Parents 88
ACT/SAT prep 29, 66, 83, 110, 129, 151, 185
Admissions notifications 201

B
Branding
    Activities 170
    Personal 126
    Social media 123, 141

C
College check list 208
College choices
    Application pool 159
    College interests 145, 147
    College research 72, 164
    Goals 14
    Tracking spreadsheet 104
College decision 203
College email account 74
College major 61, 110, 156, 158
College tours 116, 149, 152

D
Discipline
    Consistency 121
    Introduction 21
    Motivation 38
    Organization 70
    Perseverance 89
    Time management 46

E
Early Action & Early Decision 167
Essay
    Essay practice 47, 64, 112
    Essay tips 172, 176, 194, 197
    Supplemental essays 175
Everything you do matters 41
Extracurricular activities
    Activity involvement 49, 143
    Develop your passion 138
    Logging activities 54
    Summer programs 57, 63, 64, 104, 120, 147, 150, 153

G
GPA
    College 219
    GPA calculation 32
    Recalculation 217
Grade review 217
Grit 20
    Extracurricular activities 53
    Perseverance 89

H
Help
　Asking for 144

I
Interview strategies 177

L
Leadership 49, 52, 103, 143, 169
Learner 22, 96, 133, 137, 213

M
Mental health 44
　Julia Says 44, 80, 142, 154, 183, 201, 214
Mindset of excellence 39

O
Ownership shift 33

P
Planning
　Building a plan 34
　College level 219
　Goals 14
　Requirements 17
　Roadmap 18

R
Reading
　A way of life 184
　Reading challenge 29, 82, 128, 184
　Reading for fun 26, 81, 127
Recommendation letters 187
　Deadlines 199
Relationships
　Building relationships 139
　College 216

Resumé
　Future resumé 60
　Resumé tips 122, 165

S
Scholarship
　ACT/SAT 69
　College prep courses 101
　Community service 50
　Demonstrated passion 139
　Extracurricular activities 53
　Financial aid 73, 162, 196
　Negotiation 206
　Recommendation 192, 199
　Resources 114, 164
　Sports 52
　Tips 114, 117, 120, 147, 160, 170, 185, 186, 199, 220
　Tracking spreadsheet 108, 200
Social media
　Branding 141
　College tour 150, 153
　Footprint 122, 180
　Limitations 28
Study groups 136

T
Transcript 151, 201, 209
　Counselor report 188
　Finish strong 185

W
Why
　ACT/SAT prep 84
　As a learner 134
　Planning 38
　Study groups 137
　The power of 19

Made in the USA
Monee, IL
31 May 2021